Praise for Rick Mars

Dr. Rick Mars, an award-winning educator, brings his passion for patient care to life in the pages of *The Big Smile*. This humor-filled take on the modern practice is a must-read for every dentist and patient who wishes to optimize their dental care experience.

—Joe Hogan
President/CEO, Align Technology

Dr. Rick Mars *gets it* and *lives it*! Originally inspired as a young boy by working at his dad's drapery shop, in *The Big Smile* he takes you behind the curtain into what it takes to be successful in today's dental practice, at home and in your community.

—Gary Kadi
CEO and founder, NextLevel Practice
Author of *Million Dollar Dentistry* and *Dentistry for Millennials*
Documentarian of *Say Ahh: The Cavity in Healthcare Reform*

Since November 1970 (when Dr. Mars was only seven years old), I have received excellent dental care, along with three generations of my family, from the Dental Care Group. I have known Rick Mars since he was a young boy with dreams of becoming a dentist and he has been my dentist for his entire career. With his management skills and technology, he has built one of the largest dental practices in South Florida. Rick is a great dentist, a great administrator, a great teacher, a great human being, and a great friend.

—Steven Kravitz
Dental Care Group's first patient

T0145881

The
BIG
SMILE

The
BIG
SMILE

The Principles of Modern Dentistry —
for Dentists *and* Patients

RICK A. MARS, DDS

Published by Advantage, Charleston, South Carolina.
Member of Advantage Media Group.

ADVANTAGE is a registered trademark, and the Advantage colophon is a trademark of Advantage Media Group, Inc.

Printed in the United States of America.

10 9 8 7 6 5 4 3 2 1

ISBN: 978-1-64225-077-0
LCCN: 2011000000

Cover design by Jamie Wise.
Layout design by Matthew Morse.

This publication is designed to provide accurate and authoritative information in regard to the subject matter covered. It is sold with the understanding that the publisher is not engaged in rendering legal, accounting, or other professional services. If legal advice or other expert assistance is required, the services of a competent professional person should be sought.

 Advantage Media Group is proud to be a part of the Tree Neutral® program. Tree Neutral offsets the number of trees consumed in the production and printing of this book by taking proactive steps such as planting trees in direct proportion to the number of trees used to print books. To learn more about Tree Neutral, please visit **www.treeneutral.com**.

Advantage Media Group is a publisher of business, self-improvement, and professional development books and online learning. We help entrepreneurs, business leaders, and professionals share their Stories, Passion, and Knowledge to help others Learn & Grow. Do you have a manuscript or book idea that you would like us to consider for publishing? Please visit **advantagefamily.com** or call **1.866.775.1696**.

To my awesome wife, Alison, and my three incredible sons, Zachary, Blake, and Cory. You have always been there to support me every step of the way. You are my world! I love you.

To my parents, Beverly and Bill Mars, who made me the man I am today and forbade me from becoming a drapery man.

To all of the world-class team members at the Dental Care Group over the years who have been there every step of the way of this wonderful professional journey.

Lastly, thank you to my literary team of proofreaders: Alison, my beautiful wife and journalism major; Faith, my sister, the reader; and Bob Cook, my favorite all-time teacher from North Miami Beach Senior High (I am hoping for an A on this project).

CONTENTS

Introduction

Patients often ask me how long I have been with the Dental Care Group. I simply answer, "Since I was nine years old." They laugh, until I explain that I started as a patient in my own dental office when I was nine years old. Of course, I was not a dentist at the time, just a fourth-grade boy with a crew cut—a really short crew cut. Every dentist has their story. As you can imagine, my journey to becoming a practicing dentist was not typical. When I graduated dental school, most of my peers either hung up their own shingles or interviewed for jobs in other practices. I took a different path.

When I was growing up, my dad owned Mars Drapery and Upholstery on 163rd Street in North Miami Beach, Florida. My friends used to tease me that my dad's logo (a planet with rings around it) made it seem like Mars had rings, but everyone knew that the only planet with rings was Saturn. Boy, did I have a laugh years later when scientists discovered that Mars had rings around it too! My dad, like most parents, always wanted his children to do better than him in life, especially in their work lives. He told me I should consider a future profession that "wouldn't give you the same headaches that I have as a small business owner." He often talked about how everything in his business was dependent on him and how he had to always be there because no one could make decisions without him.

Besides sweeping the sidewalks as an eight-year-old, spending a year as a ball boy at the local city tennis courts, and working one summer as a lifeguard at the Marco Polo Hotel, my primary vocation during my school years was at Mars Drapery. My dad taught me so many life lessons in the twenty-two years that he was with me. In his shop, I learned to work with my hands for long hours and never shy away from a tough job. Even though I was the boss's son, I was always the low man on the totem pole, so no dirty job was ever too dirty. But most importantly, my dad taught me how to relate to and work alongside people from all walks of life with respect. He showed me how to laugh and enjoy life. My dad lived by the credo that the customer was always right, except, of course, when they were wrong. I only hope that I can convey a fraction of these lessons to my three sons. But thanks to my dad, draperies were not in my future.

Right down the street from Mars Drapery, there was a kosher-style deli called Sam's Delicatessen. One day, when my dad was at Sam's, he met a young dentist named Dr. Miles Kuttler. They hit it off, so my dad decided that we should move our family from our current dentist to Dr. Kuttler's office. In my dad's mind, dentistry would be a great profession for me, as I wouldn't have those headaches he had (a classic example of "the grass is always greener"). Dentistry seemed like a very good fit for me, as I always wanted to work with my hands. I never wanted to be the type of doctor that had to be on call 24/7, and I didn't want to confront death or dying on a daily basis.

Dr. Kuttler opened up his doors to me not just as a patient but as a mentor. During high school, I occasionally helped out around his office after school, and I frequently helped out during summer and winter breaks. I loved watching him work with his hands and seeing the things he did in very small spaces. Every procedure was like surgery. As I watched him work, he'd give me little tips and advice to help guide my journey to becoming a dentist. Many of those lessons have stuck with me to this day.

After spending time with Dr. Kuttler, I was even more convinced this was the right profession for me. I thought, *It's clean* (not like doing construction work outside in ninety-five-degree South Florida weather), *and he seems to have a very nice lifestyle* (he had pictures of his vacations in his office and drove a classic Corvette to work). Dentistry didn't involve any of the headaches my dad wanted me to avoid, like customers that made getting their draperies by Friday a life-or-death issue. Dr. Kuttler told me, "Study hard and when you get out of school, I'll have a job for you." That was a pretty bold promise considering I was only fifteen years old.

While I was in college, I went into his office during term breaks. During my visits, Dr. Kuttler explained the procedures in more detail.

Instead of just saying, "This is a filling," he would show me. "This is how we do a filling."

While I was in dental school, his teaching went to an even higher level. He explained different dental materials and different tricks, which really helped me out when I returned to school after the breaks. Unlike many of my classmates who were seeing procedures for the first time in school, I had firsthand experience.

When I got to my third year of dental school, I requested a meeting with Dr. Kuttler. I said, "For years you've been promising me a job. I'm getting out of school in less than two years. Do you really have a job for me, or do I have to start knocking on doors looking for work?"

He answered, "Absolutely. I promised I'd have a job for you, and I will have a job for you when you graduate."

A little side note to the whole story: Our practice just celebrated a milestone anniversary. We did a video about the history of the office to show the whole team, of course filming in front of the original location of Sam's Delicatessen (it now is a check cashing store). In the video, I held a broom just like the one I used to sweep sidewalks with as an eight-year-old. The shopkeepers would pay me anywhere from fifty cents to a dollar. The local butcher, Heshie, would pay me in salami, which I ate on the spot. Dr. Kuttler was also in the video, telling the story I just wrote about how he met my father at Sam's. But there was one difference: he didn't say that he promised *me* that he'd have a position for me one day, but that he promised *my father* that he'd give me a job. My dad, who was truly my hero, never got to see me live out our dream of me becoming a dentist, as he passed away after my freshman year at Georgetown Dental School.

Dr. Kuttler is a brilliant man—an excellent dentist and an amazing businessman—but he's not an emotional person. I've never seen him express his feelings at either happy or sad occasions. Yet here we were, filming this video decades after my father had passed away, and for the first time in my entire life, I saw Dr. Kuttler brought to tears. He had to really compose himself. Dr. Kuttler kept his promise to my father. I have never forgotten this.

And so I began work at the Dental Care Group the day after I received my dental license from the State of Florida on August 29, 1988. My practice is the only practice I have ever worked in.

When I first came into the practice, Dr. Kuttler had two associate dentists working with him. After about three years in the practice, I approached him and said, "I have to start thinking about my future. I'm newly married, and at this stage of the game, I should be mapping out my life. Is there a partnership opportunity here?"

He said, "Absolutely."

We immediately put the wheels in motion, bringing in a consultant (who happened to be one of my instructors at Georgetown University School of Dentistry) to put together a partnership agreement. That was in 1992, my fourth year of practice. The other associate in the practice, Dr. Joel Glicksman, also became a partner with Dr. Kuttler at the same time. It was a great partnership. We opened a second practice. Dr. Kuttler ran most of the day-to-day operations. We grew year to year, and everyone was comfortable with their roles, as Dr. Kuttler mentored his two junior partners yet delegated to allow our professional growth. Dr. Kuttler was in his prime, and there was no reason this could not go on for years or even decades. Then one of my favorite mantras kicked in: man plans and God laughs. Dr. Kuttler had an unfortunate and untimely eye injury and immediately went out on disability never to return to chairside dentistry or as the managing partner of the Dental Care Group. Overnight I went from the youngest of three partners to the managing partner of one of the largest dental group practices in South Florida. It was one of those events you are faced with and you either step up or back down. This book would be a pamphlet instead of a book if I had chosen the latter.

To this day, Dr. Glicksman and I are the remaining partners in the Dental Care Group. And I am proud to say you can count on one hand the conflicts that I have had with Dr. Glicksman in the last three decades. That is a great business marriage that has endured over twenty-five years.

Thirty years ago, we were a very unique dental practice because we operated with a one-stop-shop model. We had and still have all the dental specialties within our practice, under one roof. If you need a root canal, we have a root canal specialist. If you need to have gum work, we have a periodontist. Dr. Kuttler was probably one of the first dentists in the country to bring specialists into the office instead of people having to run all over town to get their dental work done. For a while he was considered a pariah to outside dental specialists, who felt entitled to his patients for oral surgery, periodontal surgery, or root canal referrals. Today, over thirty-five years later, his model is the model for most group dental practices, what Dr. Kuttler used to refer to as "a general and multispecialty group practice."

Dr. Kuttler was a very innovative, advanced dentist and savvy businessman, always looking into new opportunities. In 1994, he proposed opening another office in Pembroke Pines, Florida. All four of us (we brought on another partner for a short time) drove out to the location. We came to an empty construction site where they were grading the dirt before construction. None of us had ever driven that far west, almost to the outskirts of the Florida Everglades, considering our other office is a five-minute drive from the Atlantic Ocean. We looked around and wondered how people were really going to live way out there. There was nothing there! This was at the very beginning of a westward expansion in Broward County, Florida. That office is now located in the most prime area in South Florida in terms of population and growth. Dr. Kuttler had the foresight to build there before the building boom hit western Broward County.

As I mentioned, in 1996, Dr. Kuttler had an accident that injured his eye, forcing him to retire early and take disability. He left the three of us to run the three practices, but he still remains a patient to this day. I became the managing partner of the practices the day he retired and have been in that position for more than twenty-five years. Along with running the offices, I have always chosen to remain a full-time "wet-fingered" dentist, which breaks the current trend. Most managing partners of group practices with multiple offices either practice part time or retire from chairside dentistry. I am not willing to do this, as I truly love what I do. I love both my patients and my team at the Dental Care Group.

In 1998, while we were running the two locations, an opportunity for a third location came along. Dr. Jack Berne, North Miami Beach's most established pediatric dentist, was looking to move his office to a better location in Aventura, Florida. A buyout agreement was arranged with him where we eventually brought his practice into ours. (Coincidentally, Dr. Berne's office used to be located on the same street as Mars Drapery and Upholstery, also about two hundred feet from Sam's Delicatessen! It's a small world after all.)

The English word maven is defined as "an expert in the field." It is derived from the Yiddish word *meyvn*, which means "a person who understands." According to vocabulary.com, "But to be a *maven* you have to more than just understand a topic, you have to know its ins and outs. Often mavens are the people that you turn to as experts in a field. You don't become a maven overnight. That kind of expertise comes with an accumulation of knowledge over the years." After thirty years in practice, it's fair to say I have evolved into a maven of sorts. As an educator, I believe that I have the credentials to become a professor at the local dental school if I choose to be (maybe one day). But with my current schedule, I don't have the time to do it, nor do I want to leave the chair full time at this stage of my career. I love being a dentist, but I also love speaking, teaching, and entertaining people. This book seemed to me the next logical step in my career.

It's funny that when I tell people I am writing a book, I get the same response. "Really, what are you writing about?" I often answer "gynecology" prior to giving the real answer. I get it; they hope it is not dentistry, as only dentists would read a book about dentistry, and only a certain type of dentist would read a book about dentistry. I have to admit that I have read only a handful of books on the subject of dentistry since graduating in 1988, but I felt there is a great need for a book like *The Big Smile*. This book is an insider's guide to the modern dental practice. Remember the green curtain in *The Wizard of Oz*, where Dorothy thought she was seeing one thing but behind the curtain was something else? We have a metaphorical green curtain in dentistry that prevents patients and doctors from really seeing each other clearly. This book is my attempt to peel back that green curtain (as only the son of a drapery man can) and give readers an inside view of a modern dental practice, which is at its core patient centered. A patient-centered practice is founded upon healthy relationships between doctors and patients but also the relationship between doctors and their teams.

I envision this book as a handbook for both dentists and patients. I hope that by reading it every dentist can become better and patients can have a better experience when visiting their dentists. By educating both my peers and patients, I will have accomplished my first goal.

By pulling back the green curtain, in the first section of this book I hope to remind my peers that we're blessed to serve in this profession. I'm having the roof done on my building right now. With all due respect to anyone who works outside in warm weather climates, if you paid me ten times my salary, I could not stand on the roof in ninety-five-degree weather day in and day out. And I'm pretty sure most roofers don't get paid what the average dentist gets paid. We are very well compensated to change people's lives, put smiles on their faces, save teeth, and even save people's lives. That's something worth getting up for in the morning!

In the second section of the book, I want to help patients develop healthy relationships with their dentists—relationships built on trust. If patients can't trust their dentists, maybe their dentists aren't worth trusting. This book will also assist patients by letting them know if it's time to go somewhere else for their dental care. This is the reason that I chose to write a book that applies to patients and dentists and not write two separate books. I hope dentists read the patient sections and vice versa, as this would provide the optimal educational experience.

My second goal with this book: to put smiles on the readers' faces. I think there's a part of me that always wanted to be a stand-up comedian, but it was never something I pursued. I was always the class clown. I love having a good time, and I have always gotten immense joy making people laugh. Let's just hope for your sake that I am just as funny in print as I am in person.

I started speaking publicly in very small groups early in my practice, before we had our children's dental practice, Dental Care Group Kids. The first place that I started public speaking was at the Hollywood Memorial Hospital. There I spoke to pregnant mothers about dental care for themselves and for their infants. As an icebreaker, to get their attention, I started those lectures with the same line: "Okay let's go around the room and everybody tell how you got pregnant." It was a nice icebreaker and got people laughing, even though a couple women actually decided to share how they got pregnant!

I am very involved in my synagogue and was a two-time president of Beth Torah Congregation in North Miami Beach. That's how public speaking got very serious for me. You see, the synagogue president must follow the Rabbi at every bar mitzvah or bat mitzvah and say something meaningful to the child on their big day. I'd spend hours many Saturday mornings getting to know the thirteen-year-old boy or girl so I could figure out what I was going to say. This may not seem like such a huge challenge, but as I mentioned, the Rabbi gave his presentation first. Fifty percent of the time, the Rabbi would somehow say the exact same thing I was planning to say! That left me about six seconds to come up with a whole new spiel. This really taught me how to think on my feet.

On top of that, the president of Beth Torah must give an annual address to a congregation of about two thousand people. This was what prepared me for speaking on behalf of Invisalign. By talking to a few thousand Jewish people (who wouldn't be eating for the next twenty-six hours) at the beginning of Yom Kippur, I learned how to be really entertaining if I wanted to keep their attention! Talk about a tough crowd!

As I mentioned, I love to put smiles on people's faces, and public speaking for Invisalign (Align) has also given me a forum to do that. In 2003, I became an Invisalign provider. I looked at Invisalign and saw the benefits—not just cosmetic but health—of this clear aligner system that actually moved teeth. I brought it to my dental practice and my patients and decided to put my focus on it.

When Invisalign representatives visited my office, they noted a couple of things: one, they saw that I was committed to making Invisalign a vital part of my practice, and two, they saw my personality in terms of how I talked with my patients and made them comfortable. They asked me if I had an interest in teaching Invisalign to my peers by giving a couple of lectures. I said, "Sure, sounds like fun." Until then, I never imagined myself standing in front of a classroom. I was always too busy. Not to mention, I was the guy in class who sat in the back and made fun of the instructors and never envisioned that the tables would ever be turned.

Invisalign has an informal policy that you don't lecture in your own backyard because technically your audience could be your competition. There are Invisalign providers that refuse to lecture in their backyards, and I've always found that interesting because my theory is that I'm my own competition. If I do a good job, there could be dentists literally across the street from me that I wouldn't even know were there. (There actually are, and I'll talk more about that in chapter 5.)

Invisalign offered to send me to Costa Rica to teach what's called a Study Club. I went a couple of times to Costa Rica, and in addition to having fun zip-lining, it was a great public speaking experience. Then Invisalign asked if I would be interested in joining its National Faculty in 2013, which was really a big honor because I would be one of only twenty-five members in the United States. I agreed, and Invisalign put me, a guy from Miami, Florida, on the road to lecture in Tulsa, Oklahoma, and Oklahoma City to evaluate my skills. Somehow I passed the test.

In 2018 Invisalign formed the Align Global Faculty (Align Technology is the parent company of Invisalign), as they wanted to foster their worldwide presence. I was one of six dentists from the United States asked to join the original Align Global Faculty. Then in 2019, I was honored as I became one of five general dentists given the status of Master Faculty, and I was even more humbled as I was chosen as the "Educator of the Year" for the entire general dentist faculty. I have many a dental school classmate (many who have become my Invisalign students) who would agree that I have come a long way from the back rows at Georgetown Dental School.

Invisalign was right: my dental credentials have given me a knowledge base to share with my peers, and my personality has made it fun. If I finish a lecture and I don't get applause at the end of my lecture, I am almost insulted. To date, it has never happened, so if you hear me speak and no one is applauding at the end, please get it going! Invisalign has informed me that I rate very high as a speaker, but for me, that thirty-second applause is all I really need.

Therefore, the one rule that I always follow whenever I speak, be it at a funeral, an Invisalign lecture, or when addressing my team, is that I must put smiles on the listeners' faces. This is why my two goals with this book, to educate and entertain my peers and patients, are equally important. Enjoy the journey as I always say! I hope you learn a lot from my book and that it makes you smile and maybe even laugh out loud.

(Mostly) for Dentists

Chapter 1

First Impressions of Your Office

How you feel when you open up the door to your office in the morning is probably very similar to how you feel when you wake up. I'm not talking about the aches and pains you might feel when you get out of bed, but rather your attitude and mind-set. That's what this chapter is about. In a metaphorical sense, is the sun shining for you when you wake up in the morning? I can tell you the sun shines for me every single day. Some days it just shines a little brighter, but it always shines. If you're thinking the sun doesn't shine every single day when you get up, you have a problem with your mind-set, more specifically your attitude. Often when I lecture, I post a quote from famed Boston Red Sox player Wade Boggs. Wade said, "A positive attitude causes a chain reaction of positive thoughts, events, and outcomes. It is a catalyst, and it sparks extraordinary results." If you don't believe this, think of all the successful and happy people that you know, and more often than not, a positive attitude is a common trait in these individuals.

I consult for practice management and Invisalign by visiting other dentists' offices to train them and their teams. I recently spoke to a dentist in Philadelphia who said, "You must have heard of Doctor

So-and-So." I hadn't. He said, "He's the guy in town that does Invisalign for half price. He's killing everybody." The attitude of the doctor on the phone was poor at best. He lost the game before kickoff. I explained to him that Doctor So-and-So can come to my town all he wants, because all he's doing is a lot of second-rate Invisalign cases and not making any money. Patients will see right through his "dental mill." I explained to him that my patients come to me for so much more than pricing alone, so why would I worry about some other dentist that I have no control over? I never look over my shoulder. I know I am my own competition, and I recognize the things that I can control and the things that I cannot control, and I rarely concern myself with the things that I cannot control.

What someone else does is a nonfactor as to how you feel when you get up in the morning; it shouldn't be your concern. You have a whole audience of patients in front of you all day long, so why would you worry about some other dentist?

When I get to my office, I am absolutely not concerned about anything else happening anywhere else. When I put my hand on that door handle, I feel happy no matter what day of the week it is. I recently noticed an error on my schedule that showed I had appointments on a Saturday when I don't usually work that day. Instead of freaking out, my mind-set was so excited to go to work and do good things. (This is not to say that I am not concerned about scheduling errors.) I often catch myself and remind myself of the big picture. I'm fortunate to do the things I do and make a good living. What I did *not* do is move my entire schedule to accommodate my own preference for not working on Saturday. We rarely move patients in our office, because this goes against being a patient-centered office, which we will talk about more in the scheduling section of chapter 5. Mark that one down, docs. *Never move your patients unless it is absolutely unavoidable.* They book a certain time to fit their schedules, so unless they are flexible and are happy to move their appointments, don't move them except when it is an absolute emergency.

Whenever I start an introductory course for new Invisalign doctors, I ask the entire room, "What are you passionate about?" The answers vary across the spectrum. The top answers are my family, my dog, travel, and food. Rarely do I hear somebody say "dentistry." I tell the audience that my goal for the lecture is that if I would ask them that question in the future, dentistry will at least gain an honorable mention. If I'm able to inspire people with the excitement that I have for what I do, then I've done a good job. Bottom line: Love what you do, or learn to love what you do.

Loving what you do has a lot to do with establishing healthy relationships with your patients.

Healthy relationships with your patients come down to trust. It's important to get to know your patients and develop healthy relationships with them so they will understand where you're coming from and trust you're doing the right thing. We need to know about the patient, what makes them tick, and what's going on in their lives. "Why?" you may ask. Because that information often plays a major factor in determining their treatment.

While we can't have deep personal relationships with all of our patients, we need to connect on some level with every one of them that walks in the door. I will not treat strangers. On the other hand, if I'm a patient, I don't want my doctor to be a stranger either. It's important for doctors to know something about every patient and for patients to know about their doctors.

When I walk into a room, I introduce myself as Rick Mars. I never introduce myself as "Doctor Mars." I wasn't born a doctor, I'm not going to die a doctor, and I want patients to know that I'm a regular guy. Just because I wear a white coat and survived four years of dental school doesn't make me any better or more important. Anyone can buy a white coat on the internet or at their local uniform store. Doctors who truly believe that they are better than everyone else will have terrible relationships with their patients and their team—period! This may sound like People Skills 101, but you can't imagine how many dentists fall into this trap.

When I sit down with a new patient, I start with "Tell me about you." They always start talking about their dental problems. I say, "No. Not your mouth. I can figure out what's going on in your mouth in about two minutes. Tell me about you."

They typically say, "Oh, okay. What do you want to know? I'm married. I have two kids. Blah, blah, blah."

I generally follow up with a slightly deeper level of conversation. "What do you do for fun? Where are you from?"

Oftentimes the patients will turn it around and ask, "Tell me about you, Doctor." They may ask about my children. "Tell me about the boys. Where are they now?" I love that because those patients get it. They're not just there for that slam-bam-take-care-of-my-dentistry-I-gotta-go type of visit. Great dentistry is not just a product; it's an experience.

In a patient-centered office, our patients are like family. My patients are a part of my life. I was at a funeral for a patient's eighty-five-year-old father the other day. I had just returned from vacation and was heading into a short week, but I didn't care how busy I was. I had to be there for this patient. When this patient saw me, his face lit up. He knew how busy I was and truly appreciated me taking the time in the middle of the day to be there. All of our patients have come to expect it, and I do my best not to let them down. You are not going to be able to be there for every patient, but I certainly give it my best effort whenever possible. There's a saying that goes, *A parent is only as happy as their least happy child.* As dentists, the mood of our day is often dictated by the happiness of our least happy patient. I do my best to make my patients happy both in and out of my office.

I have a patient named Cindy, who is a very unique individual. She's in her sixties but a very youthful sixties. Recently Cindy's mom passed away. Her mother was probably one of the top psychics in the world and used to be called by police detectives to help solve crimes. She wasn't one of those meet-you-in-a-dark-alley-to-read-your-palm type of psychics. She was the real deal.

Cindy came by the office to say hi. She asked me, "Should I buy another mountain bike?"

"You already have a great mountain bike, Cindy. You don't need to buy another. How many can you ride at once?"

"You're right." She joked with me, "Will you buy me a mountain bike, Dr. Mars?"

I answered her, "No, Cindy. But I'll buy you flowers and lunch."

There were flowers in the office somebody had brought in, so I grabbed one from the bouquet and gave it to her. My staff ran out and grabbed her a spicy chicken sandwich, which is her favorite. That was more meaningful to her and a lot less expensive than if I had gone and bought her a mountain bike. She shared with me that people were trying to take advantage of her because she inherited her mom's money.

I reassured her, saying, "Cindy, your mom left a couple of us on the planet to keep an eye on you when she's gone, and that's what we're here to do. We'll help you out, and we already do."

We want to exceed our patients' expectations! Patients often bring their children to their appointments right after they've picked them up from school. If I hear the children didn't get a snack, I'll ask one of my team members to run out and get them food to make that parent's life a little bit easier. By the way, if I am buying, all bets are off—candy, McDonald's, or even ice cream is what they get. I want their children happy like I want my children happy. And selfishly, if their children are happy, the parents are happy, and we are guaranteed to have a much better dental appointment.

Our patients count on us for support, and they know that we're part of their lives and part of their families' lives. We almost never say no to anything when it involves our patients. Any *reasonable* request will be satisfied.

We need to know our patients enough to know they want those little, tiny things that make them happy and cost us nothing, except the time it takes to be conscientious. In our practice the patients have come to expect that level of attention from us. If we don't deliver, that's what is unexpected. And again, please don't misinterpret my message; we don't always deliver, and sometimes we receive unrealistic requests, just like you do, but we continue to do everything in our power to deliver and be the friendliest office in our city.

We've developed very special relationships with our longtime patients in that we go with them through life. I've had patients that started in my chair as children. We've watched them go through high school and college, get married, have babies, and then come back into our office with their babies because they want us to see them. (We don't want to just see pictures of the babies; we want to see the babies!) This is just one example of how we know that we've developed healthy relationships with our patients.

TRUST RELATIONSHIPS ARE A TWO-WAY STREET. (PATIENTS, PAY ATTENTION!)

We've talked about the importance of a trusting relationship between doctors and patients. If a patient trusts the doctor, then they know that the doctor is always doing the best for them. But make no mistake: trust is a two-way street. Doctors need to also trust their patients.

One patient, whom I've known for many years, had the last appointment before lunch. In a dental office, this is not a good appointment in terms of possible wait time. (Patients, take note.) If we get backed up in the morning, we're usually backed up until lunch and often use a shortened lunch break to catch up on the morning.

She came into the office in a big rush and told my receptionist that she needed to pick up her mother's headstone for her funeral. She carried on about how she absolutely had to be seen immediately. Unfortunately I was backed up and was doing the best I could to get to her. She walked out of the office. While in her car, she called my hygienist to tell her about how horrible and disrespectful it was that she had to wait for me. She kept calling my office for the next fifteen minutes, complaining to multiple team members. It was a mess, not to mention whoever started the rumor that dentists or doctors make their patients wait to disrespect them could not be more wrong.

When I finally got her on the phone, I found out that her mother had died eleven months ago, not yesterday as she wanted everyone in the office to think. She was simply having an unveiling for her mother and had a very busy schedule with family coming to town. She then started referencing unrelated things, such as how she had spoken to a friend who is also dentist, and her friend didn't think she needed to do the procedure I recommended. I got a strong feeling that she was still lying so that she could justify carrying on for no apparent reason.

The situation totally compromised the balance of our entire relationship. The issue was no longer about her trusting me but was about me trusting her. I lost confidence in this patient, not believing anything she said. The way I raised my kids was that if you lie once, you're a liar.

This applies to doctors with patients but not the other way around. A doctor, if that doctor is dishonest with a patient, can never recoup that relationship. The patient will go somewhere else. As for the aforementioned patient, she can eventually recoup her relationship with me, but that does mean I know that the patient has the potential to stretch the truth again. Doctors can be more forgiving than patients can. Trust is the backbone of the doctor–patient relationship, so why break it? It's better for patients to just be honest with their doctors.

As healthcare providers, we know that dentistry can be very expensive. People will pay very good money for things they value. Patients look for dentists whom they know and trust. A good dentist will give them 110 percent to keep that relationship. While doctors need to gain their patients' trust, patients have an equal responsibility to convey trust to their healthcare providers.

BE A MAVEN AND A *MENSCH.*

In my introduction I mentioned the word *maven*, which in Yiddish means "an expert," or a "person of integrity and honor." According to Leo Rosten, the Yiddish *maven* and author of *The Joys of Yiddish*, a "*mensch*" is "someone to admire and emulate, someone of noble character." Someone who is a maven is at the top of their game. Nowadays, our patients expect us to be mavens of dentistry. We have to be definite in our answers. If we're not sure, we should never give an incorrect answer but instead get the correct answer for the patient.

A really good friend of mine was seeing a doctor who couldn't come up with an answer for a minor problem that he was having. It wasn't minor to him, and he wanted a solution. His doctor referred him out to another doctor. That's what we need to do with our patients. If we don't know the answer, we tell the patient we need to ask a colleague to weigh in, as no one can be expected to have all of the answers all of the time. In a modern dental practice, hopefully that colleague is down the hall from you, whether it's an oral surgeon, a periodontist, or a root canal specialist. The important thing is to give the patient the correct answer.

The trouble with being a maven is that you might believe this means your first name is now "Doctor." If this is you, you will not be successful. That's what some in the medical profession call a *surgeon mentality* (no offense meant to surgeons). Surgeons often have terrible reputations (often unjustified) because people think surgeons are so important they don't need a bedside manner. That's wrong. All medical professionals, no matter how big of a maven they are, need proper bedside or chairside manners.

Dentists in particular need to be able to treat people above and beyond because almost all of our patients are in an environment that they don't want to be in. For that reason alone, at our offices, we should do everything in our power to make a patient's dental experience as positive as possible.

If you can treat people above and beyond, in Yiddish, you are what we call a *mensch*, which translated means "a very good person." Being called a mensch is the ultimate compliment. My father was a mensch. He was the person who taught me how to treat people right. Once, my father was driving with my brother Gary in the back seat. They saw a barefoot homeless man begging for money.

My father turned to my brother and said, "Give me your shoes."

Gary replied, "Seriously?"

"Yeah," he insisted. "Give me your shoes."

The homeless man was closer in size to my brother, so he gave the man my brother's shoes! That was the type of person my father was.

If somebody couldn't pay for their curtains in my father's shop, he would give them over for free or give them a break on the price. My father would even go to other synagogues that he was not a member of and give in a very quiet, low-key way by donating his services, be it curtains for the ark or upholstery for their chairs. People in synagogues often announce their gifts or how much they give. This is done for several reasons, but most often to motivate other members to give charity like their fellow members. Despite the importance of this, my father's humbleness prevented him from ever announcing his gifts publicly. He was one of those people who gave because it made him feel good. He didn't want the attention or praise.

On the Jewish holiday Rosh Hashanah we have an important prayer called the *Haftorah*, which is a short reading in the synagogue from the Prophets in the Torah. I've been given this honor for many years. After I gave the reading this year, someone came up to me and said, "Your *zaide* [grandfather] would be proud." Another person said, "Your dad is smiling at you right now. You're a mensch just like your father." That was the greatest compliment anybody could give me—calling me a mensch like my father.

> *"...in business there's a time to be nice and there's a time to be tough, but at the end of the day, you always do the right thing."*

My father taught me how to be a mensch—what was right and wrong. I believe I learned from him that in business there's a time to be nice and there's a time to be tough, but at the end of the day, you always do the right thing.

Rabbi Mario Rojzman, my Rabbi, is truly a mensch. He is the type of guy who if somebody says to him "nice tie," he'll take off his tie and hand it to them. My Rabbi has a "trick" he does when he goes out to dinner with people, no matter how much money they have. He excuses himself to the bathroom. Then he secretly hands the waiter his credit card and says, "The bill is on me. Don't even bring it out to the table." That's how my Rabbi is, yet he always turns to me and says, "I did the Rick Mars Thing." The truth is that this is a truly nice statement, but he's the real mensch. Still, it's a very big compliment to me because he's somebody I look up to. He always does the right thing. I cannot stress how important it is that we all have someone who we look to as a moral compass, be it a relative, a friend, or a religious leader.

A maven is an expert. A mensch is somebody good to the core. In a modern dental practice, you should be both. One way to be both a mensch and a maven is to use your expertise to help the community. My friend and local community leader Mike Segal recently quoted his mentor who told him "nobody ever went broke giving charity." When we give back as dentists, we get back, but not in a monetary sense. We get paid back in smiles.

In my practice we gave away our millionth dollar in free dentistry last year. Whenever I speak publicly, I always include a slide of my team holding up balloons with numbers on them that read "$1,000,000" to represent this important milestone. The funny story behind this slide is that it was photoshopped. On the day of the picture, we went out and bought the numbered balloons. As we were holding up the balloons for the picture, one of the balloons popped right before the picture was taken, changing the amount to read "$100,000." It was eight o'clock on a Sunday morning, and there was no way we could get another balloon. One of our team members went to her computer and photoshopped another balloon with a zero on it into the photo, turning the $100,000 back to $1,000,000. Now you know the secret behind the million-dollar photo.

We began our million-dollar journey seven years ago, right around Valentine's Day. Our practice held our first annual Dentistry from Our Hearts event for the community, where we gave away over $150,000 worth of free dental work to anyone in need that first year, and we've done the same thing each year since.

At the event we offer any procedure that can be done in a single day—cleanings, fillings, bondings, extractions—free of charge. We call it the hardest working day of dentistry of the year because we really hustle to see as many patients as we can before the cutoff at five o'clock in the afternoon. We also call it the best day of the year because everybody participates in the event. Our entire staff from the three practices and many people in our community volunteer. Former staff members volunteer even though some of them have moved away. We also receive contributions from some of our dental suppliers. Local restaurants donate food, the police department gives us tents, and security guards from a security company volunteer for us.

The first year we held the event, we put big signs in front of the office announcing it. I went on the radio and did interviews because I was worried no one would show up. I remember I drove by the office at midnight the night before, just to see what the setup looked like, and I saw people camping out in front of the office. I have never forgotten the message that sent to me: that people would wait through the night just to get their teeth cleaned. They continue to camp out, starting before midnight year after year.

We put our Dentistry from Our Hearts event on the news because we want the community to hear about it and come get the help they need. I also hope that other dentists will see it and do the same kind of event in their neighborhoods as well. Some patients even bring us presents to the DFOH event, such as chocolates or wine, as a kind gesture in lieu of payment. People are so appreciative. Oftentimes their luck changes, and they get jobs or insurance, and they come back and become our patients. That's the last reason why we do it, but it happens. We're just happy when people's fortunes change for the better and they can get the healthcare they need.

On the anniversary of my twenty-fifth year in dental practice, in 2013, I decided to do twenty-five free smile makeovers for the community. We held a contest called Twenty-Five Smiles where people had to write an essay and send in pictures in order to be considered for a free smile makeover. It was unbelievable how we changed people's lives. For some patients we made dentures, others received implants, and we even did a free Invisalign case on one patient! It was very meaningful but difficult because we received hundreds of applications and could only pick twenty-five. Since we could only provide twenty-five smile makeovers, anyone who we were unable to treat we directed toward dental clinics where they could get work done either for free or for a nominal fee. It's nice to know that we can change people's lives. Patients take a lot of pride in our practice because they want their dentists to help the community and give back. I can honestly say that when we make our patients proud of us, it is almost like making a parent proud when you are a child. They know this separates you from other dentists, and they are proud to be your patients.

Giving back to the entire community, like a mensch, is a huge part of what we do as a modern dental practice. We give back but not in a showy way. I learned that from my father. I don't need the attention for what my office does. But when we give back publicly, we should do so as an example to our profession and to let the community know about the good work that we are doing. It is not only good for my office's image but good for the image of dentistry as a whole.

THINK LOCALLY AND THINK GLOBALLY.

To have the right attitude and mind-set for a modern dental practice, you must also think globally. The world has changed, and we are now exposed to so many diverse viewpoints. We should all be open-minded and accepting. I am very sensitive and respectful to different cultures or opinions.

Dentists should not force their politics on patients. I don't talk politics or preach religion to my patients, especially in our current political climate. I won't put any political signs on my office front lawn. Those are my personal views. We don't even put on Fox or CNN in our reception area, because we know that we will upset 50 percent of our patients either way. We put on HGTV or Food Network. In that arena we want to stay neutral. I don't want somebody walking in my reception area in Aventura, Florida, seeing Fox News or CNN on the television because that's what the last patient had on, and saying, "I can't believe you have that on in your waiting area."

No one wants to hear excuses.

We have a wide range of magazines in our office: *People*, *US*, and *Sports Illustrated*. One thing that patients will not find is a magazine that makes them think, *Wow. I can't believe they have this magazine in here.* We don't want to do anything to offend any patients. Whether a patient is Jewish, Christian, white, black, Asian—it doesn't matter. I'm there to provide services to people, do the best job I can, and that's where the message ends.

> *The point is be humble and act decent and respectful to everybody.*

HANDLE A BAD DAY LIKE A MENSCH.

Try thinking about a bad day at work you had recently. No matter what, always remember, it all comes down to your patients. No matter how bad your day is, you have to stop and think about them.

I'll tell you about a horrible day I had when I was running late. It seemed like every single one of my patients was upset that day because I was behind in my schedule *and* the patients somehow all scheduled themselves too tightly. I'm not expecting people to block off six hours in their schedules when they visit the dentist, but if they have a ten o'clock dentist appointment, they shouldn't book their next appointment somewhere else at ten thirty or even eleven. On that day it would have been nice if my patients had left a little cushion where if something happened and the doctor was running late (which I was), they wouldn't become overly upset. That is a note to all patients in a dental office.

On this day I reminded myself I didn't have to be wrong to appear wrong in my patient's eyes. What mattered is how I dealt with the situation. I handled it like a mensch: I was apologetic to my patients. Just as important, I did not make excuses. No one wants to hear excuses. As Gary Kadi from Next Level Practice taught me, "An excuse is a well-planned lie." Sounds harsh but think about it. An excuse might be legit, but it means nothing, as it does not change a thing. An apology at least shows you care and respect your patient.

One patient in particular had to wait an hour, and he became very angry. He threw his bib at the front desk. A lot of doctors would have said, "The guy threw his bib? I would have told him to get the hell out of my office and never come back again!" But that's not me. I wanted to try to make it right. I might not succeed, but I was at least going to try.

I called him immediately after he left the office. First, I apologized. Then I let him know in no uncertain terms, "Don't you throw your bib in my office because that's not acceptable." I told him, "I'm a patient like you are. I wait an hour at doctor's offices sometimes, too, but I understand what doctors go through." I pointed out to him, "To the best of my knowledge, you're not a doctor, and you don't know what it's like to be a dentist." He apologized and explained that he was under tremendous work pressure and would be more understanding in the future.

Conversely some people feel that if they're upset, they're going to get satisfaction only if they can get under your skin and get you just as upset as them. Something Dr. Kuttler told me was "Sometimes they just want a pound of flesh." You know what? We're not a butcher shop. You want a pound of flesh? Go buy a steak. In those cases where a patient is completely unreasonable and disrespectful, your best option is often to part ways and unfortunately make someone else's life miserable, not yours.

The point is be humble and act decent and respectful to everybody. Be a mensch. Act like the "regular" guy or girl that you are to your employees and to your team. I'm the type of person that comes in and shows everybody my pimples. Not literally, of course, but what I mean is that I don't come across like my "shit doesn't stink." I don't want my team to think I have that perspective. I want my team to say, "We love Dr. Mars. We look up to him. He's a great guy. But he's a regular guy too. He falls down just like everyone else, and he gets up. He doesn't walk around like his life is absolutely perfect. He tells us the good, the bad, and the ugly."

When I walked in my office the next morning, I told everybody what happened. I said, "Look at all the things we do for our patients. We can't park in our parking lot because we give them our parking spaces. We just beautified our reception area. We have HGTV on and not CNN. We give them water bottles, blankets, headphones, and even Wi-Fi. None of it mattered yesterday because I was running late. Our patients didn't care about anything but me running late."

That was the lesson, that timeliness is a big factor in what patients think about us. Going forward, I have a new mind-set. I don't care what it takes, but we are going to do everything in our power to run on time, no matter what. And just as important, *no excuses*, as most patients do not care. All they care about is that you are late and they have to wait.

No matter how bad your day is, it could probably be worse. I remember treating a patient on 9/11. The Twin Towers were knocked down, the White House was being "attacked," and Jeff was in the middle of a dental procedure. He was sure that his child's Jewish day school (in Florida) was going to be the next institution under attack in this country. Meanwhile, I'm trying to perform a filling on him. It's not that I didn't feel compassion for Jeff. It's that I was trying to finish a distoocclusal filling on tooth #2 during one of the worst hours in our country's history—clearly a bad, horrible day. My point in light of the events on 9/11: realize what a truly bad day is, whether you're a doctor or a patient. What we think is a bad day might actually just be an okay day with one not-great moment. There's a big difference.

Every day I walk into the office in a good mood, and I almost always walk out in a good mood, too, because sometimes people are just going to be miserable no matter what. What I always say to myself is "I only get that miserable person for half an hour or an hour every six months, but they have to deal with themselves 24/7, 365 days a year." I'm going to walk out of my office smiling at the end of the day. I'm not going to let one unhappy person ruin it. If a person doesn't like to laugh, that person is not my typical patient. In fact I recently dismissed a patient because she had no sense of humor. (This is a story, dear reader, I will have to tell you in person if we ever meet, as it is too fresh.)

Too many bad things in the world can legitimately ruin your day. Running a little bit late is not worth ruining it. If a patient has to wait a while for you, then they should be very happy that's the worst part of their day. But that does not mean you should not apologize immediately and acknowledge that you respect your patient's time.

In our next chapter, I'm going to ask you to put yourself in your patient's shoes and think more about patient-centered care. When you walk through your door as a patient, what is your very first impression of your own office?

Chapter 2

Walking into the Modern Dental Practice

What's the feeling that you get from your office when you walk in the front door? Before you answer that question, walk into your office as a patient and look around. Are your magazines outdated? Are the bulbs burned out? Do you see dust built up in the corner? Are your air-conditioning units putting black marks on your ceilings? Even though a modern dental practice goes beyond just the physical, your physical space is still reflective of your culture.

What our practice looks like today is much different than how it looked ten years ago. It looks night-and-day different from how it looked twenty years ago. If we had a patient walk into our office today who hadn't seen us in twenty years, that person would be blown away. No windows at the reception desk, modern decor that is updated every couple of years, and a warm, friendly attitude greet you as soon as you enter any of our offices.

We're constantly looking to improve. My team knows one of the worst things you could say to me is "Nothing ever changes around here." This is because everything is always changing around here. We're getting

We're getting better by trying new things.

better by trying new things. Sometimes they don't work, but that doesn't mean we're afraid to try them.

BE INTENTIONAL ABOUT MODERNIZING YOUR DENTAL PRACTICE.

I think one of the biggest mistakes that somebody can make when they establish their new office is to do it just like everybody else. A practice opening up next to a retirement community will be very different from one opening up next to an elementary school. I think your office has to reflect you and your patients. If you have a modern house and you're a modern person, why shouldn't your office reflect your taste? If you're a traditionalist, maybe your office will look different, but regardless, it should express who and what you stand for.

I have a good friend, Dr. Clarke Sanders, who unfortunately experienced a fire at his office and his practice burned down many years ago. He wrote about it in his book *Fired-Up Dentistry*. When it came time to rebuild, he decided to do it better, physically, but more importantly, and operationally. That's exactly what he did, and it was a turning point in his career. Going to work became much more rewarding, not just financially but emotionally. What happened to him is unfortunate, but he turned a bad experience into a win. The point here is: Why should you wait for your building to burn down to do things better? Why not start now?

Sometimes you need a little help, so don't be afraid to reach out to somebody more knowledgeable. We've brought a number of consultants to our practice over the years. Some consultants only got us to a certain point before teetering off, and others we took a risk on and didn't get everything we wanted. Regardless, they all helped transform our practice over the years in varying degrees.

In each of our three offices, we've created very warm, welcoming environments for our patients. You know the frosted glass window and bell that most doctors still have in their offices? The day we took our windows down and rebuilt the front desks in our offices marked a very different era.

Our entire office is a very open space. All of the operatories (with the exception of our pediatric *quiet rooms*) are open. For patients who may be nervous about dental care, this creates a more transparent environment. They aren't trapped in a windowless room and kept worrying about when someone will come in. With open operatories, patients can see us walking by. Oftentimes I'll pop my head in the room and say, "Hey Larry! I'll be just a couple of minutes," just to give a heads-up and put the patient at ease.

In a modern dental practice, the reception décor should be current and new. That doesn't necessarily mean that it must look contemporary because again, some dentists like more of a conservative look, but it needs to be fresh. Your office should never look tired, with worn out furniture and dingy walls. You've got to repaint your office every couple of years and replace old furniture.

If something is worn out, repair or replace it immediately because you don't get a second chance to make a good impression. If you have light bulbs out in your reception area, patients will notice and wonder why you're not paying attention. If I see that a light bulb is out, I'll go change it myself if no one else is available. Your magazines should never be outdated either. We spend a tremendous amount of money on publications our patients want to read. When I walk into a doctor's office and see a one-year-old magazine with crumpled up corners, I know that the doctor doesn't care enough about his patients to invest in the patient experience. I have deselected several physicians because of outdated magazines and shabby office décor. Bottom line, patients often come to your office to improve their smiles, so your office space should look good and reflect both your taste and skill.

I recently was at the University of Miami seeing the department chief for an annual checkup. I sat in the reception area for an hour. I understood the doctor's delay, but while I sat in the treatment room alone, I noticed there was no television, not a single magazine, and not even a Wi-Fi connection. I stared at the walls for another hour. I brought this to the department chief's attention, and he was mortified and assured me this would be corrected. It made me want to write a book about patient care (so here it is).

It's our job as doctors to scrutinize our offices at a higher level than our patients. My staff has been trained to be very attentive to those details because I may not walk out into my reception area every day. We have a cleaning service come in every night, but again, my staff knows to watch for extra things. If somebody has a beverage in the reception area or leaves a newspaper behind, my staff immediately picks it up because the next patient who walks in won't know that somebody had just left it. They might assume that we don't keep our reception area clean. We are mindful that we only have one shot with patients.

Our patients have come to expect a high level of comfort and cleanliness from our offices. We recently remodeled our reception area. It was a major overhaul and a large expense. The feedback we got from every patient that walked through the door was very positive.

In terms of the money spent on the remodel, we get a high return on that investment because our patients keep coming back. Our patients see the attention to detail in all aspects, not just the décor in our office. They are proud and happy with the remodel, as this is *their* dental office. We're coming off the best year we've ever had, which is not a coincidence. When you invest back into your practice, it comes back to you in spades.

That being said, don't spend on huge recurring-cost items that you alone think are aesthetic. These kinds of things might even come across as too showy to patients. One example is a very expensive fish tank, which a lot of doctors have. They cost a fortune to put in and maintain. In my humble opinion, it's not worth the expense, as your patients see them for just a couple of minutes. Some doctors argue how relaxing they are, saying it sets the mood. I say get your patients in on time, and your patients will be in a good mood. Make them wait and stare at a fish tank for an hour, and they are going to hate those fish!

BE SMART ABOUT YOUR EQUIPMENT AND MATERIALS.

We've discussed keeping patients comfortable in the physical office environment, but the equipment you use plays an equally important role. When it comes to choosing equipment for a dental office, doctors really need to do their homework. New equipment is constantly coming out, and it's very expensive.

Dentists like technology. If it has bells and whistles and looks good, sometimes we just can't resist. The problem is, if doctors aren't properly trained on new expensive equipment, it ends up gathering dust on the shelves or in the corner of your storage closet. That's a bad investment. In the modern dental office, while cutting-edge equipment is essential, it also must be a smart investment.

> *In the modern dental office, while cutting-edge equipment is essential, it also must be a smart investment.*

I've surveyed other doctors on technological advancements over the years and asked what the big game changers were for them. Most agree that the advent of digital radiographs changed everything. In terms of financial output, digital X-rays pay for themselves over time because we save a fortune on chemicals and film. In terms of treatment, the images are high resolution, so we can see cavities at a very early stage. In terms of patient comfort, this allows us to do conservative restorations often-times without using the dreaded needle.

Another great example is digital scanners, such as the iTero scanner from Invisalign. Instead of spending money on impression material, we now have very accurate scanners that replace those mushy impressions that no patient ever liked, especially since assistants and dentists often have to take impressions several times to get it just right. On an Invisalign patient's first visit, in minutes, the iTero scanner provides a simulation of what they are going to look like following their Invisalign treatment. Digital dentistry is here. Doctors know it, and patients demand it from their dentists, as they should.

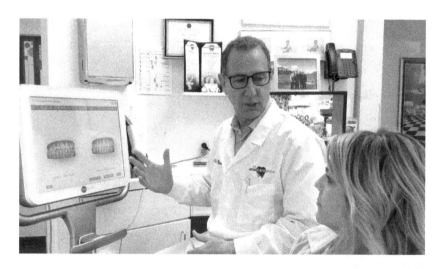

If your machines are always breaking down and the X-rays are poor quality, then there's no justification for not switching over to digital. It's the same thing with scanners. While I'm lecturing, some doctors hear the scanner costs upward of $25,000 and they say to me, "No way. I can't spend that money." I tell them to call their assistants up and ask, "How much did we spend on impression material last year?" They hear the number, and they're embarrassed because they had no idea where all the money was going.

In my practice, we've learned about smart purchasing through trial and error. At one point we purchased a towel warmer so we could give warm towels to patients. Think about it. If somebody hands you a warm towel, as if you're in a fancy restaurant, you're going to wipe your hands on it. The problem was that the towel was for their faces! After seeing this and watching the patients' reactions, it dawned on me: *Here we are in South Florida. Somehow, they sold us a towel warmer.* Towel warmers became an office joke—code for useless gadgets. I don't even know where the towel warmer went to. Eventually we started giving cold bottled water to our patients because that was what they wanted when they walked in the door from the ninety-degree heat and 100 percent humidity, not a warm towel. Little tweaks like that can make a huge difference in the patient experience.

Other than the towel warmer, we have very few things that we've purchased over the years that gather dust. Twenty years ago, we bought one of the early lasers, but it paid for itself over time. It provided a very good service to patients even though it was our first very expensive, $50,000 piece of equipment. A second laser we bought for considerably less was purchased for cavity detection by measuring tooth density. It provides early detection, like digital radiographs, allowing my doctors to consistently determine if occlusal caries are present. It takes the guesswork out of determining if a stain is a deep groove or true caries and often detects caries when they are not detectable through radiographs or clinical diagnosis. We also have CT scans in our office that help our oral surgeons and periodontists place implants with increased accuracy. These are investments that allow us to provide optimal care to our patients. Do they know it? Maybe, but we know it, and in this case, that is most important.

With expensive dental equipment, unfortunately, there are very few discounts. Sometimes there are promotions, but inexpensive quality dental equipment just doesn't exist. That's because suppliers know doctors can and will pay, and they capitalize on that demand. It's our job to do our homework by going to dental meetings and looking at the equipment and products, talking to doctors who use them, and using our common sense.

Talk to your patients as well. We have a device in the office called the Wand. It's a computer-generated anesthetic system. Many years ago I had a patient ask me about it because she had heard about it on the news.

She asked, "Do you have the Wand?"

I answered, "I don't."

She said, "Well, I'm new to the area. I really like you. I insisted that my previous dentist in Texas get the Wand. He did, and I have not had a painful injection since. If you can get the Wand, I'll stay your patient. If you can't, I have to find a doctor that has it."

I immediately thought, *Wow. This is a great patient testimonial. Let me go find out about it.* I brought in a representative so I could see the Wand for myself. Almost every dentist would agree that the most painful injection in dentistry is the dreaded *palatal injection*. The Wand rep claimed that patients barely feel a palatal injection after using this piece of equipment. My sister, Faith, who was working for me at the time, jumped in the chair and said, "Okay. Give me a palatal."

Nobody in their right mind would ask for that (except my sister), but I used the Wand and gave her a palatal. She said, "That was nothing. I didn't feel that at all." I ordered three machines that day, and I've been using them ever since.

We not only use the Wand to provide patients more comfort, but in our offices we place a solution known as sodium bicarbonate in the anesthetic. It's called "buffering the anesthetic." It takes away the sting when a patient gets an injection. We tell the patients we're doing this because if we don't share with them the lengths that we go to for their comfort, patients won't know how much we care about them.

Equipment costs are factored into the cost of dental treatment, which is something that patients aren't always aware of. If patients knew that a new dental chair costs anywhere from $10,000 to $25,000 or that a CT scan costs over $100,000, it would help them to understand why quality dental care is expensive.

Patients have no idea about the quality of the materials being put in their mouths unless we educate them. There were some dentists who, to save a few dollars, sent their crowns to China. In fact some are still doing this. The crowns they got back from China often contained lead. Patients had no idea this was going on, but doctors and dental journals knew about it. Bottom line: Never cut corners when it comes to quality care. It will come back to bite you every time, as it should.

Our patients pay more for comfort and for quality. We use zirconium crowns that are stronger than metal on our patients' posterior teeth. I've never had one break on a patient, and I've put in thousands. We use very aesthetic porcelains on the anterior teeth because we're in an affluent area and have a demanding patient pool that say the porcelains better not show a margin and better match "perfectly." When I have completed an aesthetic procedure, I hand the mirror to these patients, and they put it three inches away from their teeth (as most of your patients do), though no other human will ever view their teeth that close. But for them, it has to look good from three inches away, or we do it again.

DO THE RIGHT THING BY YOUR PATIENTS.

A big turning point in my career is when I realized that I didn't need to make money on every patient. I need to do the right thing for a patient and sometimes money doesn't factor in. If I put in a crown and it's not perfect enough to go into my own mouth, it doesn't go in the patient's mouth. Even though it costs me more money to do another scan and send it back to the laboratory, I'll do whatever it takes. I will even replace a crown that is a year old if I see a radiograph from a different angle that shows a less-than-ideal margin or if I detect a light contact from shifting.

I'm not concerned with the financial aspect of doing the right thing.

If I'm doing an Invisalign case, and if the patient has reasonable expectations or if I'm not happy with the results, I will keep refining the case until we get satisfactory results. I will keep doing the right thing. I'm not concerned with the financial aspect of doing the right thing. I'm only concerned with doing the right thing. Period.

Here's an example of a nondental ethical business practice: I pay an HVAC company to come to my house every two or three months to clean my three air-conditioning units. A technician came to my house and told me there was muck in all the units and that the filters were all dirty. Apparently, they had been doing a lousy job. When he was checking the unit in my attic, he triggered the sensor, which caused it to leak. The unit leaked through to my fire alarm, which set my fire alarm off at two o'clock in the morning. My wife and I woke up, and it was raining on us inside the house from the leak in the air-conditioning unit.

The next day I called up and spoke to the service manager. He said, "Oh. Okay. We'll come out today to clean it."

I said, "Whoa, whoa, whoa. Wait a second. Do you understand something? He came to look at one unit. He did something wrong to the other unit. I'm a really good customer. I have three dental offices that you service. I have a house that you come to every few months. This happened because of you guys, no matter what you say." I continued,

"Jon, one of two things will happen. I'm going to pay you because I have no choice but to fix this, but you'll never step foot in my house or businesses again, or you'll do the right thing. You're responsible for any damage from this leak, and my walls are filled with water. I just painted them. I have wood floors that I just installed. Just do the right thing, and you have a customer for life."

The owner, Lee, called me back later. He said, "We cleaned everything out. Your units are immaculate now. We changed the pan that's rusted out. You're not paying for anything, Dr. Mars."

I said, "Lee, you get it."

He said, "No, I appreciate what you said to my service manager, Jon, and I took it to heart. You're 100 percent right. I don't need to make money on every single thing I do. I'll make money from my customers in the long run because I'm going to keep them happy. They trust me, and they're going to keep coming back."

I said, "Exactly." Lesson learned by Lee.

There's a legendary story about a customer who went to Nordstrom to return a tire. He brought it to the customer service desk and said, "This tire went flat on me, and I need to have it replaced. It's only a few months old."

As you're probably aware, Nordstrom doesn't sell tires. The salesperson, because they are all so well trained at Nordstrom, took the tire from the customer, went down to Sears, replaced it with a new tire, and brought it back to the customer. The customer left, thinking Nordstrom was the best store in the world.

Maybe that's going a bit too above and beyond, but the lesson is to do the right thing. Do the right thing. Do the right thing. In the modern dental practice, we do the right thing.

Now that you've thought about your practice from the patient's perspective, I'm going to ask you to take that one step further and walk through your front door as a new patient, pretending that you've never been there before. Don't just do this once, but keep doing it so you make sure that every patient, whether new or longtime, has the same amazing experience.

Chapter 3

New Patient Care

In the last chapter, I asked you to note your impressions when you walk through the front door of your practice as a doctor but, more importantly, as a patient. For this chapter, I'd like you to imagine how you feel when you first walk into a familiar place but with a totally different experience. Walk into your own office as a brand-new patient. Try it, and your eyes will be wide open, and you'll see everything in a very detailed, close-up way, almost as if under a microscope. Imagine how you would like it to smell, feel, look. Do you feel the energy and a good vibe?

This is how it feels to be a new patient in a dentist's office. In the past I have seen new patients walk in our office with their eyes scanning the room as if they're looking for snipers. In the modern dental practice, what we've learned is that the new patient experience starts even before the patient walks in the door.

IT TAKES A FRONT-OFFICE TEAM TO CARE FOR A NEW PATIENT ...

I'll walk you through the new patient experience as if you were a new patient at our office so that you can get an idea of how it's done in a modern dental practice. With new and old patients, our office takes a team approach where everybody plays a role.

Your new patient experience starts on the telephone before you arrive at the office. If you aren't handled right, you're not likely going to show up. We often use that as a measuring stick. If the people answering our phones are doing a good job, there is no reason why new patients shouldn't show up. We go to great lengths to train the people answering our phones so that they are efficient and pleasant. Here is a rule to live by: *new patients are never put on hold when they call.* No exceptions.

As I have mentioned, we do everything in our power not to create any obstacles for new patients. If you call and we offer you a Tuesday morning or Thursday afternoon appointment, we're still available if you ask to come in on Wednesday, even if there is no available appointment. We'll let you come in on Wednesday and take a tour of the office and fill out the new patient forms. Then you can come back another day that works for everybody. We don't ever want to say no to new patients. Of course we let patients know that this is a "meet and greet appointment," and should they prefer a visit with the doctor, we arrange another appointment for their comprehensive new patient visit.

There is another method we use to ensure new patients show up to their dental appointments. All of our doctors personally call all of their new patients the night before they come into the office to say hello. Our doctors do this to break the ice because a new patient has no idea whom they will meet when they walk in the door. You could have picked me out of an insurance book or a friend could have told you about me. My call the night before sets the tone for when you come the next day. It's also a reminder to come to your appointment. Think about it. When was the last time a doctor called you for anything, espe-

> Here is a rule to live by: *new patients are never put on hold when they call.* No exceptions.

46

cially just to welcome you to their office? You're less likely to forget to show up when the doctor calls you to confirm. I also call new patients to get them excited about coming to the office. Many of them say, "I can't wait to come into your office!" Who says that about a doctor's office or a dentist's office? I might also remind you to do your registration online, before coming to the office.

When you enter our office, we know who you are. Someone from my front-office team comes out to where you are seated and greets you either formally or informally, depending on your preference. They'll say, "Welcome to Dental Care Group, Charlie. How are you doing today? Come on in. We are ready for you now."

I went to a dermatologist once, and I waited an hour and twenty minutes. The nurse came to the door, and how do you think she greeted me? She said, "Mars!" Not "Dr. Mars." Not "Rick Mars." Not even "Mr. Mars." Just "Mars." I was mortified. In our office, we go out and physically greet the patients whether they are new or are longtime established patients. Right away, we give patients a warm welcome and feeling in our practice because we care.

As a new guest, you're given a tour of the office, usually by the treatment coordinator. While you are on your tour, everyone in the back is very attentive and greets you as you're walking through. I meet patients all day long who are in the office to see other doctors, but if I greet them in a friendly way and they need something else down the line, they're going to think, *I remember Dr. Mars. He's a nice guy.*

In addition to giving our patients a warm, welcoming feeling, let me share with you another important reason we greet you as we do. Let me take you back to the worst night of my life. This was unfortunately when my father was rushed to the hospital because he had a seizure. He eventually died from a related medical issue. When I was in the emergency room, I will never forget that my friend's father, who was a doctor working there, saw me. He turned his back and walked away. I thought, *I will never ever do that to anybody, anywhere.* Nobody, patient or otherwise, would ever say that we're inattentive in my office. We go way above and beyond.

The new patient experience continues when a dental assistant provides the patients with what we call our "Comfort Menu." On the Comfort Menu are a broad spectrum of things that you can have to keep you happy and comfortable during your visit, including blankets, bottled water, and headphones so you can listen to your music while in the chair. And yes, we do have Wi-Fi in all of our offices.

When you are in the hygiene chair, as a new patient, you also receive a gift—that's right, a gift—which is always something cool, such as a Dental Care Group phone charger. Our team then proceeds with a short interview followed by any necessary radiographs. The patient is then screened by the hygienist. One of our dentists then enters the treatment area and provides a definitive treatment plan.

… AND IT TAKES A BACK-OFFICE TEAM TO CARE FOR A NEW PATIENT.

As a new patient, you don't see a lot of the back-office moving parts. We have assistants in the hygiene room who maintain the treatment rooms and assist with radiographs. This allows our hygiene team the time to not only clean your teeth and keep your gums healthy but to educate you.

After you see the dentist, you again meet with the treatment coordinator, who reviews your insurance to advise you of which portion, if any, is your responsibility. The *only* person in the office who talks about finances with you is the treatment coordinator.

The treatment coordinator will help set up different financial options for you depending on the treatment. As a modern practice, we help you figure out a way. We offer interest-free financing options, or you can spread the fee out over longer payment plans. When you prepay for your treatment with a check, credit card, or cash you also receive a 5 percent "pay today" courtesy.

Our modern dental practice back office runs like Disneyland with their FastPass. We've taken away the lines, the waiting, and the inconvenience. There's a chair at our front desk where the phones almost never ring and where you can sit down and talk to someone when you want to check out. But you won't need to because all of your future appointments are made in the treatment rooms. The only reason to stop at the front desk is if you haven't prepaid your treatment, which is rare.

WHAT HAPPENS WHEN YOU'RE NOT NEW ANYMORE.

I'm fifty-six years old and have been practicing for thirty-one years, which really feels like two blinks. Everything I just wrote about the new patient experience has evolved from trial and error. We offer new patients the VIP treatment, but that never stops. Why blow you away that first visit to have you one day ask, "How come nobody has offered me a bottle of water since 2014?"

I have a longtime patient named Rob. Once while he was up in the Berkshires on vacation, he broke a tooth. He made an emergency visit to a dentist in Massachusetts. When he returned, he told my hygienist and me, "This was some office I was at for my emergency in the Berkshires! This guy had cameras in his office and took pictures of my teeth!"

I said, "Rob, we have cameras too."

He asked, "How come I've never seen them?"

My hygienist and I both looked at each other. We knew right then and there that we dropped the ball on one of our longest-standing patients in the office. We never bothered to impress Rob like we had impressed the new patients. I stuck my tail between my legs, and that day it became very clear to me that we can't rest on our laurels.

We live, and we learn by our mistakes. What I learned is that existing patients have to be treated as well as new patients. We constantly have to keep earning their respect.

There's a great old United Airlines commercial that I show my team every couple of years, which you can find on YouTube. In the commercial, the executives are having a meeting in a conference room and the CEO announces that they just got fired from their oldest client after twenty years because he said he didn't know them anymore. They were bemoaning the fact that "We used to do business with a handshake." But now they do business through their phones and fax machines. That's how old the commercial is.

The CEO walks around the room, handing out airline tickets. He says, "We're going to go back to the way we *were* doing business. Face-to-face meetings and touching all of our customers."

At the end of the commercial, someone asks the CEO, "Hey Ben, who are you going to visit?" He answers, "I'm going to visit that old customer."

I've shown that to my team countless times so that they know that we always have to remain personable. We always have to understand our patient's needs.

Steve is the longest-running patient in our office. His mother, also a patient, died recently. I went to her funeral. Do you know how busy my day was for me to run out and get to the funeral? I literally had somebody pick me up from my office to go to the funeral, and afterward my wife drove me back to the office. I had people waiting for me and things I had to do, but I knew I had to be there for Steve. Steve was Dr. Kuttler's best man at his wedding. He was there the day that the doors opened on the office. He's continued to be a loyal patient. His son is also a patient—the third generation. Steve's whole family comes because he trusts us. He knows that we're not going to make a bad decision for him.

We're going to do only what's best for him. And we are going to be there for him, like he has been there for us for almost fifty years.

By entering your office not once but often, as if you're a new patient, you can really understand what the patient experience is like. This will help you make any needed changes to how you and your front and back office run. Remember, no matter how new or old a patient is, it's important that they receive VIP treatment before, during, and after they leave your office.

PUT EVERY PATIENT'S NEEDS FIRST.

Our journey to becoming a patient-centered office started on the phone and moved right into our parking lot—that's right, our parking lot. Early on, we would shrug when patients came in and said, "You don't have any parking in your office." We'd say, "Sorry, but that's a good thing for us because it means we're a busy office." Then we started to realize we could do that better. Now we don't even let our team park in our parking lot. Our whole philosophy has shifted to caring about the patient: making it about our patients, not about our doctors or our team.

The greatest feature of a modern practice is stopping and thinking about your patients and putting their needs first. Here's an example: I'm a person who loves air-conditioning, but other people get cold very easily. We have a twenty-two-year-old patient that every time she walks in the door, she's wearing a sweatshirt, and it's ninety-five degrees outside! We have a blanket ready for her as soon as she sits in the chair. This patient feels like she's the VIP of the Dental Care Group. Little does she know, so does the patient in the room next door because that patient likes to have a water bottle waiting for them as soon as they walk in. And the patient who likes to have ESPN on the television—he has the remote control ready for him. If we're really on our game, we have ESPN already on when he walks into the office. You would not think people would show up to their dentist's office on their birthday, but they do. And if that happens, watch out. You'll find balloons aplenty, and every available staff member sings "Happy Birthday." You better believe patients share that experience with all of their friends.

I need to reiterate that the key to any successful modern dental practice is that your patients' needs come first. Take the time to get

HOW ARE YOU DOING IN YOUR PRACTICE? HERE IS AN EASY EXERCISE …

You can always hire a top-notch consultant because there are some great ones out there in the dental field, but here is a simple, easy way to improve your practice in no time at all. Poll your team. That's it. It is probably best if done anonymously. In your morning huddle, ask your team to identify the one thing they would improve about your practice (and it cannot involve raises). By the end of the day, ask them to drop their suggestions in a suggestion box. You will be amazed by the great feedback that you get. Do this regularly every six to twelve months.

to know what they like, and be sure that you provide that top-notch personal service for every one of your patients. This way they know you don't just care about their mouths but that you care about their entire well-being.

While I can never stop talking about the patient, I need to bring the next chapter back around to you, the doctors. Did you know that we are America's unsung heroes? Our responsibility goes beyond the lips and teeth. We are not just dentists—we are doctors of the mouth!

Chapter 4

Dentists Are America's Unsung Healthcare Heroes

The CEO of *Next Level Practice* and a friend of mine, Gary Kadi, wrote a book several years ago with the title *The Dentist: America's Unsung Healthcare Hero*. Most patients wouldn't describe their dentists as *heroes*. But the truth is, most patients don't realize that their dentists could save their lives. Think about it: most people only go to their physicians when they get really sick. Only a small segment of the population keeps their annual checkup appointments. On the other hand, most people see their dentist twice a year in order to get their teeth cleaned. Given that frequency, dentists are by default given the responsibility of not just being dentists but being doctors of the mouth.

WE ARE DOCTORS OF THE MOUTH.

Even though we are the "doctors of the mouth," a dentist's responsibility for their patients' health goes beyond the teeth. For example, in my practice we do blood pressure checks on all of our patients at least once a year. Each patient is screened for oral cancer. We do saliva tests to detect eleven different types of plaque or bacteria that indicate risk for heart disease, stroke, or diabetes. Also, our radiographs can even reveal blocked carotid arteries. Dentistry in the twenty-first century looks very different from "your mom and dad's dentist."

That being said, many dentists refuse to take their patients' blood pressure or do saliva testing for bacteria or HPV in their offices. Many believe that by doing these things, they're accepting responsibility that they don't need or want. But I would challenge them with the question, What happens if a patient has a heart attack and asks you, "How come you didn't catch that? What was my blood pressure?" If I could help one dentist make a single fundamental change, this would be what I would advise. Simply take your patient's blood pressure at least once a year.

If I could help one dentist make a single fundamental change, this would be what I would advise. Simply take your patient's blood pressure at least once a year.

We've had many patients in our office whose blood pressure is outside the normal range and rather than treating them, we've sent them to urgent care, the ER, or immediately to their physicians. Those patients have come back and thanked us for catching it and helping them. More importantly, I can honestly say there are multiple lives that have been saved in our practice, which is priceless! Docs, take note that the majority of the patients that we find with abnormally high blood pressure have not seen their physician in quite some time!

Over the course of my career, I have seen numerous patients where we've found dangerous plaque and bacteria in their mouths after they've had illnesses, and we wished we could have seen them and gotten them help before they became sick.

Although physicians and dentists do receive the same general medical training the first two years of graduate school, physicians are leery when it comes to working inside a patient's mouth. They may take a look around, but they're certainly not going to fabricate appliances and take impressions any more than we would perform pulmonary surgery on our patients. Even so, dentists should take advantage of anything and everything that falls under our umbrella. Make no mistake, I am not suggesting that we do the physician's job, yet we certainly can become level one screening for patients who have not had regular medical checkups.

Our unique knowledge gives us the ability to work with physicians so that they will treat the patient the most efficient and best way. We should be better educated and stay current with our training. For example, in my practice we work with physicians to diagnose sleep apnea and make appliances to help keep patients' airways unobstructed when they sleep. If we have an Invisalign patient with sleep apnea, we structure the retainers to give the patient a greater airway space.

We have so many valuable diagnostic tools in our office that are all for the patient's well-being. In spite of this, patients become leery when they feel like they're being upsold. They ask themselves, *Why is my dentist doing this?* The tests that we're doing in our practice set us apart from most dental practices, but more importantly, the tests can save lives. The revenue from these tests does not make or break our practice financially. In fact the tests don't affect our bottom line. All we are doing is providing potentially lifesaving services to our patients.

As doctors of the mouth, we have to understand that we see people twice a year, regularly, and we have to take advantage of these opportunities to optimize and protect our patients' overall health. If we miss an opportunity, it could cost a patient their life. On the other hand, if we can catch things early enough, we can absolutely save lives. Be heroes!

CAN'T YOU JUST GIVE ME A CLEANING?

No new patient ever comes into the office and says, "I need to get a full evaluation with radiographs, have my blood pressure taken, and get a good deep scaling." But they do come in on the first visit and say, "I just need a cleaning." We hear this almost daily. We always inform new patients that the first appointment is, pending an emergency or something unusual, for a full evaluation and not a cleaning.

It's the right thing because just cleaning teeth to get new patients does nobody a service. This is like putting blinders on. You may not catch something until (and if) you get another opportunity to do a full evaluation on that patient. Dentists, as doctors of the mouth, have an obligation to their patients to do the right thing, not the quick and easy thing just to get a new patient.

Patients tend to gravitate toward dentists that prescribe the least amount of treatment. These unscrupulous dentists do this knowing that more treatment will be necessary once the patient is established in their office. This puts patients at risk, as when they are not treated in a timely manner, their conditions progress. Then they need more extensive and expensive treatments.

I had a friend from high school who came to my office several years ago as a new patient with a fractured palatal cusp (the portion of an upper tooth closes to the roof of the mouth) on tooth #12, approximately two millimeters below the gum line. The correct treatment plan was an extraction, an implant, and a crown. He decided to seek a second opinion from an unethical doctor. That was my friend's last visit to our office, as the new doctor said he would "save" his tooth. I noticed a new crown in my friend's mouth at a social gathering about a month later. I never discussed this with my friend, nor did he mention it to me. About two years later, I noticed my friend was now missing tooth #12 and was walking around without any temporary. I wasn't surprised, but I was mortified. I don't think it ever occurred to my friend what happened. The treating doctor and I are the only ones who know that he did not keep my friend's best interest in mind when treating him. The more "appealing" treatment plan (the one with a less complicated treatment) cost my friend about $3,000–$4,000 on top of the cost of the implant and crown. Patients need to ask the right questions so they know that the least amount of treatment today is not always the best treatment. In other words, the least amount of treatment presented to a patient is often not the best treatment for a patient. Finances are often a factor in a patient's decision to accept treatment, but it should not be the primary factor when deciding on treatment options. Oftentimes it's like that old Fram oil filter commercial: *You can pay me now or you can pay me later.*

It's better to have patients that understand our philosophy and how much we care about doing the right thing rather than others who are looking to get in and out the door. If a patient puts their health first, there's no issue. In the modern dental practice, our first job is to educate and often inspire patients so they can appreciate what we're trying to do and trust that it's the right thing.

If you're doing the right thing, then stick to your guns.

In my practice, when patients say, "I just want to have my teeth cleaned," we hand a form to them and say, "Why don't you look this over, and we'll explain it to you?" The form tells them that cleaning is a preventative procedure, not a therapeutic procedure, and it protects them from gum disease.

Sometimes, patients just don't want to hear it. They'll fight you on it or even walk out of your office, but if you're doing the right thing, then stick to your guns. Don't ever give a patient the "wrong" treatment. We take our Hippocratic Oath promising *not to do harm. Doing harm* is just giving somebody a cleaning when they need to have more. It's better to lose a patient than to "undertreat" the patient just to keep the patient happy and in your office.

If every single doctor in this country stood by their guns and did the right thing when it came to new patients, patients would have no choice but to receive the proper treatment. But unfortunately, a lot of doctors are just looking to get that warm body in the door, so they give the patient what they want, rather than educating them and giving them what they need and deserve.

We've had numerous patients over the years become very combative with us when it comes to the issue of "I just want to have a cleaning," but we're willing to fight that good fight. All of us in dentistry should be willing to fight that good fight to educate and inspire our patients and stick to our guns with the proper treatment. In the end everybody wins when we do that: our practices, our profession, and above all, our patients.

WE EDUCATE PATIENTS WITH THE PROBLEM, CONSEQUENCE, AND SOLUTION MODEL.

The old-school model of a traditional dental practice was to tell the patient they have a problem and give them a solution. "You have a cavity. We need to do a filling." In the modern dental practice, we educate and inspire our patients by showing and explaining the problem to them, explaining the consequences of not fixing the problem, and then giving them the solution. We tell them, "You have a cavity. We show them a radiograph or a photo of the cavity and then explain, if you don't take care of the cavity, the cavity is going to get bigger. It can then turn into a root canal, or even worse, you can end up losing the tooth. Therefore, we have to treat it now with a filling before it gets out of hand and unmanageable."

Everybody on our team understands our culture: we explain to patients exactly what's involved with their treatments and answer any questions that they have. For example, the entire staff went through our sleep apnea training. We don't get educated just for our own edification. The whole reason we learn is so that the entire team can share what we know with our patients.

Realistically we have some patients that don't want to know all the consequences. "If you're saying this is what I need to have done," a small segment of the patient population says, "just go ahead and do it. You don't have to tell me or show me any radiographs or pictures or anything." Most people need to understand clearly what's happening and what's going to happen if they don't do the treatment. That's exactly what we do.

One of dentists' biggest faults is that we often skip over the consequences. The consequences are our opportunity to educate the patient. If we skip the consequences, the patient will likely skip treatment. Here's an example of a conversation devoid of consequences: I tell the patient, "You have gum disease. I'll send you to the hygienist for four quadrants of scaling and root planing. Then we need to align your teeth properly with Invisalign. Following the first phase of treatment, our periodontist will evaluate your periodontal health."

Inevitably the next question out of the patient's mouth is "How much does it cost?"

I answer, "That's about $7,000."

They respond, "I don't have $7,000. Bye. Have a good day."

When we educate the patient, the conversation goes like this: "Your gums are bleeding because you have gum disease. Let's take a look at your intra-oral photos. You're only supposed to have approximately two millimeters of pocketing around your teeth, but you have a three-, four-, five-, and even a six-millimeter pocket here. I don't know if you are aware, but gum disease has been linked to heart attack, stroke, diabetes, pancreatic cancer, and even erectile dysfunction. (By the way, ED remains the number-one attention getter of male patients, topping stroke and heart attack combined.) If you don't do something about it, you're putting yourself at a similar risk as a smoker or a person who is fifty pounds overweight." Then I move to the solution. This approach works much better, as now the patient has been educated as to the consequences of doing nothing and is more willing to be treated.

EDUCATION BUILDS TRUST WITH YOUR PATIENTS.

Both dentists and patients are partners when it comes to the patient's health and well-being. We need a willing partnership with our patients. They must be willing to accept the things that we propose so they can stay out of trouble and stay healthy for a long, long time. The only way they will is if we build their trust, which of course goes back to educating our patients.

I once had a patient come to my office who said she was there because her dentist, using the old-school model of problem and solution, told her, "You have five cavities. Let's get you scheduled for fillings next week." She was very upset. She just couldn't believe him on his word alone and wanted a second opinion. I did a full evaluation. I explained to her that I was using a device called a DIAGNOdent™. The DIAGNOdent measures the density of a tooth, reveals any soft spots, and therefore can catch cavities very early on. I found seven cavities, two more than her previous dentist, and showed her every single one of them. She left her dentist and did the treatment with us because she understood two things: one, her dentist wasn't thorough in his exam, and two, her dentist didn't take the time to show her the cavities and explain the consequences of not treating them.

That's part of our culture in our office, that we take time to do things right and educate and inspire the patient through communication and the latest technology. I love hearing a patient say at the end of a new patient exam, "I've never been to a dental office like this before. This is incredible." That means everything to me. That's how I know we're doing it right. Sometimes patients get offended when you tell them the truth, but we're going to do the right thing every single time. You're going to end up way ahead of the game when you do the right thing.

A final word on education. You may notice that I have a hard time mentioning "education" without mentioning "inspiration." Whichever term you prefer, hopefully both, know it is key to your success as America's unsung hero.

Chapter 5

Behind the Green Curtain (for Dentists and Patients)

What standards do you think patients use to evaluate their dentists? Is it, "They did a great filling on tooth #15," "The distal lingual margin on my first molar crown is exquisite," or "I have absolutely zero plaque left in my mouth after my visit"? The answer is obviously none of these.

Dentists get evaluated by very narrow criteria. Did we hurt the patient? Did the patient pay a fair price for their dental treatment? If it's cosmetic work, does it look good? Unfortunately the most important thing to most patients is, "How long did my doctor make me wait?" It seems crazy, but so many of our patients place a higher priority on wait time over quality dental care!

Be on time, and if *something happens*, be prepared.

We all have days that run like clockwork, where patients respect our time and we honor patients' appointment time. But some days things just take a little bit longer. For example, one patient's mouth (small opening, moves their tongue around a lot) is more difficult to work on. Just one patient who is a gagger or one that has difficulty getting numb can wreak havoc on a dentist's schedule. Every dentist has experienced this, yet many patients don't want to hear it.

Patients whose professions have meetings with fixed beginning and end times can't understand that our profession isn't like that. We go to great lengths to do our best to run on schedule, but as we say in dentistry, *spit happens*. Here's how I've learned to handle the spit and manage the time.

> We go to great lengths to do our best to run on schedule, but as we say in dentistry, *spit happens*.

Don't make excuses. It's that simple. If it happens that I have to take a little longer, I will never give a patient an excuse. I stopped making excuses a long time ago because people don't want them, and frankly, they don't care. Instead of an excuse, I apologize whenever I'm late. A sincere apology is the first thing that comes out of my mouth when I walk into the room (after *hello*, of course.)

When necessary, we explain how we work to our patients. Some patients have a misconception that the doctor overbooked, like an airline trying to fill seats. We explain to them that we never overbook—we never put more patients on the schedule than we can handle. Some procedures just take longer than expected. Occasionally our schedule is completely full, and a patient, for example, has an emergency and has to be seen immediately. Even if there's no space on the schedule, we have to create it for that patient. All of our patients need to understand our culture—if they have an emergency, we will make space for them, even if we have to take the heat from our other patients who must wait. We also make sure that our patients understand that if they have to wait, when it's their turn, we're going to give them the same time and quality service. We will never rush through their appointments in order to make up the time.

Schedule wisely. Doctors tend to not allow enough time for patients. In a modern dental practice, patients come first. If you're wondering,

How can I get my patients in and out the door as quickly as possible? your patients will sense that. Patients do want things to run in an efficient manner, but once they're in the chair, they want your full attention.

Oftentimes dentists fall into the trap of allotting the minimum or even the usual amount of time if everything goes perfectly with each appointment. This is also a mistake. We extended our appointment times for our patients several years ago. For example, when a patient needs a crown, we used to schedule that as a half hour to forty-five-minute appointment. Now we've extended those appointments to one hour. In a patient-centered, modern dental practice, by allotting an extra fifteen minutes per patient, we ensure patients have the attention that they need and that we have the necessary time to complete the procedure just in case everything does not go as planned. We've found our patients are happier, and we're more profitable at the end of the day.

Doctors also tend to think that patients run on their schedules instead of the other way around. This is another mistake. For example, I had planned a trip to Virginia Beach for a speaking engagement that was cancelled due to inclement weather. I was originally scheduled to return on Friday night and see patients on Saturday. Now that the trip was cancelled, I had no patients booked for Friday, but I was still scheduled to work on Saturday. I would have loved to move all my Saturday patients to Friday, but I didn't want to inconvenience all those patients. Plenty of doctors would have done so, but that's not a patient-centered attitude. I have had associate doctors in my practice insist on my team booking their schedules from the first thing in the morning until the end of the day, not when it is convenient for the patient (a.k.a. "booking up"). Small battles have ensued when I explain to the doctor that patients schedule when they can come to our office, not so you can get out early if you are not booked. I realize my model will not work for all, but with the proper guidelines, your patients will be happy and a doctor's schedule will run efficiently and profitably.

Customize select appointments. We have certain appointments that are *guaranteed no-wait appointments*. These are the first appointment of the morning and the first appointment right after lunch. Those are the appointments over which we have complete control, and we let patients know that. We reserve these times for our patients with busy schedules or for patients that hate to wait when they go to any doctor's office (like me, to be honest).

If we are delayed at all and somebody does have to wait, we'll try to let a patient know as soon as they arrive that we are backed up today. Or if we do get backed up while they're waiting, we'll let them know that we will absolutely get them in as quick as we can, but if it's an inconvenience, we'll reschedule them. Every patient is different. The other day when I was running late, I had one patient who insisted she should have been called and told I was running late, and then I had another patient who said, "You only called me an hour before and told me you were running late. That's not acceptable." You have to be sensitive to every individual's needs as long as the requests are reasonable.

Unfortunately, time, not the quality of one's dentistry, is quite often the biggest factor in how a patient weighs your worth as a dentist. And for this reason, the bottom line is dentists need to respect patients' time, and patients need to understand why their dentist may run late.

NO MORE "DRILL, FILL, AND BILL." LET'S TALK ABOUT MONEY.

Historically dentistry followed the old adage *drill, fill, and bill*. Patients went to the dentist, had a cavity drilled and filled, and were later sent the bill. It was that simple. Many dentists ended up with serious financial issues because nowhere else did any person follow a system like that one. People have never loaded their carts up at the supermarket only to inform the cashier, "Send me a bill. I'll just pay you when I pay my other bills."

Dentistry was unique, and patients came to expect that. In the 1990s, things started to change. Our profession collectively decided not to bill patients anymore, opting for the pay-for-service model. More recently, in the last ten years, third-party payees got involved, which allows patients interest-free financing to help them afford their dentistry. This is a necessary evil in our country where 65 percent of the population does not have $500 in the bank for a medical emergency.

At our office, we encourage our patients to prepay for their treatments. Prepaying is a win-win several times over. The dentist gets their money up front. They don't have to worry about their patients' roofs leaking, air-conditioners failing in the middle of summer, or their cars breaking down. Here's another win-win: if our patients prepay, they receive a discount. On our side, we've found that patients who prepay are far more likely to keep their appointments. And yet one more win-win: Prepaying takes money off the table, so our team doesn't need to have that dreaded conversation with the patients every time they come in. When patients are done with their treatments, they don't need to stop at the front desk to pay, which saves them time and cuts down on patients waiting in line to pay their dental bills, one of the most annoying experiences at a dental office.

In dentistry, patients often view the work that we do as elective. They forget about the health benefits of dentistry and how important it is. When we can take the finances out of the question and make their payments more affordable, it puts the quality work we do in the spotlight. When I present the treatment options to a patient, I often hear, "Let me see how much it costs before I start treatment."

I wrinkle up my nose and squint at them a little bit and say, "Would you have this same conversation with your cardiologist? Why do you value your oral health any differently than you value any other part of your body, especially knowing the relationship between periodontal disease and heart disease and stroke?" I add that many people have lost their lives to untreated dental infections. We share laminated articles with patients about people who have died from dental infections. We had a consultant, Judy, in our office recently who candidly shared that she had a friend who called her on a Friday with discomfort and passed away on that Sunday. We need to stress to our patients that this is not elective treatment and not "just their teeth!"

When people worry about finances, they unfortunately lose focus on what's important. We have a responsibility to make it financially easy for our patients to do the right thing.

Diane first visited my office about twenty years ago, and I hadn't seen her in a while. She came back to the practice about six months ago for Invisalign, several crowns, and to redo some veneers on her front teeth. I asked her, "Diane why did you come back to our practice after all these years?"

She answered, "You know, there was a time in my life that I couldn't afford the quality of care that your practice offers, so for routine cleanings and maintenance, I went elsewhere." She continued, "But when I knew I needed important treatments, I wouldn't let anybody else do it but you." When we hear this from our patients, it reaffirms that we are doing the right thing, and sometimes we have to battle circumstances outside our world that are beyond our control.

We hope that patients will be able to afford our services and stay with us all along. With that in mind, we try to work with everybody as best we can, but sometimes it doesn't happen. When a patient like Diane puts a high value on her dentistry and feels that we are the only ones who can provide that level of care, it is very meaningful to us. The fact that she valued her care with us was the highest compliment she could have paid us.

DON'T TALK MONEY TO YOUR PATIENTS.

In traditional dentistry, dentists discussed finances with their patients. They made financial arrangements and even negotiated deals with their patients right at the dental chair. In a modern dental practice, patients don't want a doctor to focus on money at all, as it's uncomfortable. They want their doctor to concentrate on their treatment. In our practice we agree wholeheartedly. That is why we have treatment coordinators who make all of the financial arrangements with the patients, which you will probably remember from your tour as a new patient in chapter 3.

Whether a patient does or does not accept treatment, fortunately, does not affect my lifestyle whatsoever. But whether a patient does or doesn't accept treatment, in most cases, will affect *their* lifestyle in a drastic way. I must admit, unfortunately, that this does not dissuade some patients from putting finances ahead of their oral health regardless of their financial circumstances, but an effective treatment coordinator compartmentalizes this concern, moving it out of the dental chair, where it really does not belong.

It is not uncommon for some patients to liken their interaction with the treatment coordinator to that of the finance person in a car dealership. It is customary when purchasing a car to end the experience with a visit to the finance manager, who upsells them into the undercoating, tinted windows, and other random things that add to the overall cost of the vehicle. The treatment coordinator in a modern dental practice would never do that. Nobody gets a commission if you let the doctor pull an extra tooth. Nobody has an agenda. The role of the treatment coordinator is to assist patients so that you can fit their treatments into their lifestyles. They are a key patient ally in the modern dental practice, and patients need to know this.

Treatment coordinators play another positive role with our patients when they first enter our practice. By having the treatment coordinator also greet patients and give them tours of the office, when patients sit down with them, everything feels familiar and friendly. We didn't want *car dealership finance guy* to be our treatment coordinators' personae. Their whole interaction with patients is much more open and trusting, as it should be.

IS IT OKAY TO NEGOTIATE WITH MY DENTIST?

If you have never attempted to negotiate a fee or if it has never occurred to you to do so in your dentist's office, this might seem absurd to you. That being said, some dental patients feel it is their God-given right to negotiate fees with doctors. If you are among this group, let me suggest this approach: ask the treatment coordinator in your dental provider's office what the parameters are for negotiating in that particular office. Definitely avoid financial negotiations with your dentist, as most, like me, get very uncomfortable discussing this. If you want to save money, you can always take a tentative approach with the treatment coordinator by feeling out the situation with a question like "I'm not using a credit card. Is there any way we can do better if I pay cash, check, or prepay for my treatment?"

Even if you are unable to negotiate, that's okay. Your health isn't about the money. It is about the quality of the care you receive and staying healthy. That's where your focus should be. Think of it this way: Would you negotiate with your cardiologist or urologist? Why do you feel it is okay to negotiate with your dentist?

AND DON'T WORRY ABOUT WHAT YOUR COMPETITION IS DOING.

Even though doctors shouldn't be talking about money with their patients, that doesn't mean they shouldn't be making sound business decisions behind that "green curtain." One of my specialists goes around to different offices, and he tells me how certain offices do things. I'm shocked that they aren't making sound business decisions. They give away services in their office, taking a loss to gain patients. That is not how they will grow their practices.

They'll grow their practices by doing great dentistry at a fair price and by treating patients well in a pleasant environment. There's no magic to it. We all have cycles where business is busier and then slower, but if we keep doing the right thing, making consistently honest and correct decisions, we will have happy patients at the end of the day.

But sadly, some dentists look for shortcuts with things such as Groupon or by running costly advertisements announcing drastically discounted fees. We had a local dentist who I heard was spending over a quarter of a million dollars on advertising per month! He was all over television and radio with really slick ads. Besides their own dentist, nobody knew any other dentist's name in town because he was everywhere. As it turns out, he was doing illegal things with third-party payments. Because he was taking shortcuts to get ahead, he had his license suspended, and nobody ever heard from him again. Stay true to sound business principles. Shortcuts almost never work.

Good doctors who do the right thing are the ones that stand the test of time and are successful. The point I'm trying to make is that we are not in competition with each other. We are only competing against ourselves. If you have patients in your chair and you do the right thing—you educate them and provide amazing dentistry—you will be successful. This proves my point: in New York City you can walk into an office building and see dozens of dentists on the directory. Some are more successful than others, but it has nothing to do with the proximity of their perceived competition. The dentists who succeed in that building are doing great dentistry, are treating people right, and have clean offices—these are the things that patients demand.

In a shopping plaza literally a hundred feet away from my office is another dental practice. The day that dentist opened up his office, I went by to say hello and welcome him to the neighborhood. He wasn't in the office, so I left my card. I told the front desk, "Please tell him to stop by anytime and say hello. It's nice that we get to know each other since we're right across from each other." That was over fifteen years ago, and I still have never met him. Not one of my patients have ever come from his office and vice versa. His competition factor is zero for me. If I do a bad job on a patient, they'll leave my office because I did a bad job. They won't leave my office because of another dentist right across the street.

When dentists mistakenly think that modern dentistry is all about who has more ads, better coupons, or a flashier website, they don't understand. This isn't to say that successful advertising and marketing are not important, but being successful in a modern practice is about patient-centered care. It's really that simple.

EVERYONE ON THE TEAM PITCHES IN.

The worst thing a team member could ever say in our office is "Sorry, that's not my job." We all of course have specific functions in our office, but we also know anything can be your job, within reason. If the phone happens to be ringing as you're walking by, even if you're a doctor, you need to pick up that phone if no one else is available. If there's a patient standing at our front entranceway, I'll walk over myself, greet that patient, and check them in.

This culture starts at the top. A team member in my office would never walk right by a piece of paper lying on the ground and not pick it up. They see me pick up papers, trash, or a plastic bag blowing around outside my office window all the time. That's because cleanliness in and around the office happens to be another criterion that patients measure us by. We have new patients come to our practice all the time that left their former practices, saying, "Their office was filthy. I saw blood. There was paper lying around. They didn't wash their windows." We hear that kind of feedback and respond, as it shows us how important it is to patients that our office be clean.

On a daily basis, we do things to keep the office clean. We have inspections of our bathrooms every hour. Twice a year we have a cleanup day in our office, usually on a Friday afternoon after work. Everybody on the team changes into their cleaning clothes, and we get on our hands and knees to scrub our office from floor to ceiling. We clean off the baseboards and take a toothbrush to the crevices around the operatory chairs. Although we have a cleaning service that comes into our offices every night, they don't really get into the details like we do: from removing a bug in a light fixture to lowering down an art piece that hangs fifteen feet off the ground and dusting it. It is a total team effort where every person participates, be it doctors, assistants, or hygienists. My team understands the importance of this. Cleanup day is part of our culture. We all know it demonstrates pride in our office.

In a traditional dental practice, if you told your staff that they had to stick around and clean the office, a lot of them would refuse. But we do a lot of really great things for our team, and in return they buy in, as we all share in our practices' success.

With communicable diseases, such as AIDS and hepatitis, cleanliness is a big concern to patients. I had a patient who traveled from Dubai to my office in Miami to have his dental work done. (Note: It is very humbling that we have many patients in our office that travel internationally for the quality dental care that we deliver.) This patient purchased his own dental instruments, including handpieces, because he was so concerned about sterilization. This despite the fact that I gave him a tour of my office and showed him our high standards. We have a dedicated sterilization area in all of our offices. In addition, we have a full-time sterilization technician in each office. We send off all of our sterilization equipment for spore testing to the University of Iowa. Although this patient from Dubai demanded an extremely high level of sterilization, we know that each of our patients deserves this, and we do everything in our power to provide it.

These are the details that most patients won't ask you about, but many of our patients are very observant and see how equipment is bagged and sterilized and notice how clean the office appears. My patients know that the very next patient could be my wife or child, who will be treated with the same level of care and cleanliness as them. It's a great amount of time and expense to provide this level of cleanliness, but the value and peace of mind it delivers to our patients is priceless.

THE PHONE SETS THE TONE FOR YOUR ENTIRE OFFICE.

About three years ago, we decided to be much more efficient with our phone system. We are three large offices with fifteen, eleven, and nine chairs respectively. Because of our call volumes, we had phones ringing at the front desk constantly. Patients, when they were ready to check out and leave the office, had to stand around waiting to schedule their follow-up appointments and make payments. It created a huge backlog in our office. Our patients' amazing experiences in the dental chair ended abruptly and negatively at our front desk. And their last impressions were often the ones they recalled when we surveyed our patients.

The phones also put our administrative personnel in a very bad position. They had to decide between the patient on the phone and the patient standing in front of them. We had patients walk out of our office without making appointments or paying for their treatment. We decided to solve these problems by implementing a call center that we refer to as our Patient Care Center.

Our Patient Care Center is in a centralized, dedicated area, completely away from the front desk, on the second floor of one of our offices. It's pleasant and calm. (Patients don't hear background conversations or the sound of noisy drills when they call.)

Every team member in the Patient Care Center

It takes a lot of effort to make things look effortless.

must undergo a five-star customer service training. The phone is answered in two rings or fewer. Appointment setting is quick and easy—they only ask patients for pertinent information. Doctors' messages are taken efficiently and sent electronically. If a new patient calls, the Patient Care Center never puts them on hold to take another call. When a team member is talking on the phone to a new patient in our office, they are not to be disturbed for any reason whatsoever.

We've experienced great results since making this change about three years ago. We've cut down on hold times. There is no more chaos at our front desk. The front desk personnel are fully engaged with the patients right in front of them. They're able to immediately handle any payments the patients need to make on the way out. (Most of the follow-up appointments are actually made in the treatment areas, so patients don't need to use the front desk for that anymore.) In short, the Patient Care Center has had a positive, efficient domino effect on our entire practice. With the front-office team freed up from the phones, they are available to assist patients immediately.

These are the kinds of efforts we make behind the green curtain. Patients don't realize what we're doing; they think everything runs seamlessly by itself, and they've come to expect it. But it takes a lot of effort to make things look effortless.

Most patients who change dental offices do so because of administrative staff and auxiliary personnel and not the dentist. That kills dentists because no matter how highly trained, talented, on time, or fairly priced we are, patients will leave our office because of another team member. As a team these are the outcomes that we want to avoid. By instituting a Patient Care Center in our office, we have found that we have much higher satisfaction and retention rates among our patients.

BE LIFELONG LEARNERS AND EXCELLENT COMMUNICATORS.

We always strive for better ways to keep patients happy and satisfied. When it comes to our team, a big difference between the old dental practice and the modern dental practice is education and willingness to learn. We have numerous meetings not only to keep communication open but to provide opportunities for learning and growth to our team.

Fifteen minutes before we open our office each day, we have a morning meeting, known as a huddle, to brainstorm about any issues we're having and discuss the patients of the day and any special concerns we anticipate with those patients. We also might talk about the monthly production and maintenance issues. (Our entire team is fully aware of how well the office is doing or not doing—there are no secrets.) All of our team leaders, including human resources and bookkeeping, meet every week for at least an hour. We have quarterly team meetings where we close the office and invite third-party experts in to share their knowledge as part of our team's growth and development. For example, we all might run through customer service techniques, the latest hygiene techniques/ services, or even scheduling.

Every Thursday I spend time in my office meeting with team members one-on-one to brainstorm about how to improve the practice. Our philosophy is that if we stay still, we are definitely going to fall behind. It's up to us as a team to keep striving to get better. As the "captain" of your team, you must set aside weekly time away from the chair to constantly evaluate your practice.

Our patients have grown to expect that level of service, as these meetings have paid off for them. We brainstorm about how we can better greet the patients, or we modify our delivery system to best implement a piece of beneficial technology, or we might just remind the team to make sure that we are consistently checking every patient's blood pressure. Sometimes we introduce new things to the practice, such as a new patient gift, or we bring on a new team member, or we reinforce the guidelines for sedation of our patients for surgical procedures.

In the next section, we will look at things from the patient's perspective, sharing with them some things that go on behind the green curtain in a dental practice.

For Patients

Chapter 6

How Do You Feel When You Walk into Your Dentist's Office?

The most important thing for you as a patient to feel when you walk into your dentist's office is trust. The best way to begin a healthy, trusting relationship with your dentist is for you to have an "innocent until proven guilty" mind-set. In other words, assume that you can trust your dentist unless you find a reason not to. Something to contemplate: Every doctor is a patient somewhere. We go for checkups at other doctors' offices. But very few of you, our patients, are doctors. We know what it's like to be in your position as you walk into our door, but you might not necessarily know what it's like to wear a dentist's white coat.

This is what I want to show you, the patient, in this second section of the book. My goal is to educate you so you can better understand why things cost a certain amount of money, why you might have to wait for your appointment, and why you shouldn't have a cleaning on your first visit to a dental office. I also want to impress upon you that you can be demanding of your dentist if you have a healthy, trusting relationship. On the other hand, it's important that you're fair and take responsibility for your role in the relationship—for which it helps to know all the things you can do to make your visit optimal and receive the highest level of care.

DEMAND BETTER FROM YOUR DENTISTS.

You, as the patient, have a right to demand certain things from your dentist. The first thing you should demand is that your dentist educate you about your health and your treatment. If you're unclear about a procedure, ask for an explanation or even a visual demonstration. Dentists have models of the human mouth and digital technology that we can use to make things clear. If you have questions, you need to feel like your dentist will take time to answer and explain.

The most important thing, remember, is trust.

In our practice, when a patient has a complex treatment, we might need to bring them back a second time to educate them thoroughly if we've already spent the time allotted for them that day on their exam. For example, if a patient is a reconstruction case or has severe periodontal needs, those treatments have many nuances. In those instances we would need to have them back to explain their treatment thoroughly. We'll even bring patients back a third time if they want to have their spouses or family hear exactly what's going on. We're happy to do that because we want our patients to have all the information they need to make an informed decision. We don't want patients returning in the middle of or following their treatment and saying, "I had no idea that was what was involved."

The most important thing, remember, is trust. You need to feel comfortable with your doctor. If you demand transparency, your dentist should know this is a fair demand and deliver. That is how a trusting relationship between a doctor and patient works.

A TRUSTING DOCTOR–PATIENT RELATIONSHIP IS FOUNDATIONAL FOR EXCELLENT CARE.

A trusting relationship between the doctor and the patient gets stronger over time. It takes a number of experiences in order for you to learn to trust your doctor. Unfortunately, in most cases for patients, their doctors only get one strike and they're out. One mistake can be enough for the patient to think, *There's a lot of other dentists around that I can go to. I'll find another one.*

Fortunately for patients, doctors tend to be a lot more tolerant of our patients than they are of us. That of course has something to do with the dentist being supported monetarily by our patients, but we're supporting our patients with great dentistry. This is why the trust relationship is a two-way street and why it's important that over time, doctors and patients build that relationship together.

Some patients have a misconception that because they pay large fees to their dentist, their dentist owes them more than just great dentistry. This puts a tremendous amount of strain on the doctor–patient relationship.

We want referrals based on our work alone.

A while ago we experienced something just like that. We held a drawing in our office where patients who referred their friends or family to our practice could be entered to win big prizes, such as televisions and bikes. One patient, Brody, won a fifty-five-inch flat-screen television. My staff filmed Brody the moment we told him that he won. As he was talking, his brother walked in the door and said, "I referred Brody. How come I don't get a television too?" He was serious, and that is what hurt. I think he forgot that we are here to take care of our patients' teeth, not give televisions to the whole family. We are very grateful when people refer patients to our offices, but we don't want referrals motivated by patients getting something out of it. We want referrals based on our work alone.

Now when patients refer multiple patients to our office, we keep things simple by sending them chocolate-covered strawberries, magazine subscriptions, movie tickets, or gift cards—not as incentives but as polite thank-yous. We know this is still above and beyond great dentistry, but we like to show gratitude to our patients whenever we can.

Unfortunately a small segment of the patient population might indicate, in a quasi-joking way, that their doctor owes them something because they've spent so much money at that practice. I've had patients say to me, "I paid for your new reception area/car" or "I've put your kids through college." (Usually those aren't even the patients that truly have spent a large amount on their treatments!) We know those comments are said in jest, but it really does send the wrong message to your doctor and is unhealthy for the relationship. Doctors don't owe patients anything—just like patients don't owe their doctors anything—beyond what is reasonable and customary. Doctors don't call patients and say, "Hey, you didn't send me a birthday card this year or a holiday present. I was kind of expecting that because I work so hard on you." A doctor only owes a patient quality dentistry in a pleasant, clean environment, period. Anything else is icing on the cake.

ADVOCATE FOR YOURSELF TO GET YOUR NEEDS MET.

In any kind of relationship, it's important to communicate your needs, wants, and dislikes. It's terrible when a patient leaves my practice, and I have no idea why. For me, the lion's share of the time, if I knew the reason that patient was unhappy, I could have easily rectified the situation.

Our Patient Care Center reaches out to patients if they haven't been to our office in a while. If patients tell them they are going to another dentist, they will ask why the patient left our practice. Sometimes the reason is cost, and now they are spending less money elsewhere. This is unfortunate, as they often don't realize that lower costs often mean they may not be receiving comparable materials or as high quality of service. I had one patient go to a less expensive local dentist for a crown, not realizing that their new dentist was sending his crowns overseas to China to save money on materials and that these crowns were later found to contain lead. Another patient was upset about waiting for appointments. That patient spoke up about wanting to go elsewhere and found out about those guaranteed no-wait appointments. We have solutions that can pretty much satisfy everybody, should they have an issue. We do have to know there is a problem, or we have no chance to correct the problem, and everyone loses.

You must discuss your wants, needs, and dislikes with your dentist. You might feel reluctant if you get embarrassed or think it might stir up hurt feelings. I understand that. But if you have enough trust with your doctor and are able to tell your doctor exactly what the problem is, oftentimes, that doctor can and will remedy the problem.

FEEDBACK IS A GREAT WAY TO BUILD A TRUSTING RELATIONSHIP.

When I go to a doctor's office as a patient, if I see something glaring, I feel I have an obligation to give feedback. While I was in my friend's office (also a doctor), I saw a large duplicate stack of magazines with a cover announcing the top doctors in the area. I was happy for him, as I thought he was mentioned in the article. Why else would he have a whole stack of those magazines in his office? I grabbed the first one off the stack and flipped to the section with his specialty. He wasn't even in the magazine! When I said something to him, he had no idea that those magazines were even there. I told him to recycle them, and he did. As a doctor myself, I'm apt to be more up front with another doctor, but there is no reason any patient should be reluctant to give positive feedback to their dentist.

We have people that aren't even patients give great feedback. They'll come into the office and say, "Hey, I've noticed that there is some garbage outside your garbage can in the parking lot." We are so appreciative because we care deeply about these things. Now all of our neighbors know that if they see something, they can tell us because we will do something about it.

Test your doctors to make sure that they are open to feedback. If their magazines are outdated, request that they purchase some current magazines. Or if they don't have Wi-Fi in the office, request that they purchase Wi-Fi to make your patient experience more enjoyable and see if they do anything to correct the problem. It's not unreasonable to ask your doctors to spend a few dollars more to do the right thing. After all, it's not like you want a $100,000 CT scanner for the office. (That's okay, too, in my opinion!) Watch how your doctors receive this kind of constructive criticism. It will tell you a lot about the type of doctors that you're dealing with. Which of them thanked you? And more importantly, which of them fixed it? Those that are averse to constructive criticism aren't worth your time. That's a big deal breaker in a trusting relationship. I cannot even tell you how many healthcare and business relationships I have terminated over this very issue.

If somebody gives me feedback, even if it's negative, I welcome it, and I thank them. I once had a patient call me and say, "Your receptionist was a little rude." I thanked them and said I'd take care of it. We happen to record our calls, so I played back the call in order to address the issue with the receptionist who spoke to the patient. Whenever I receive any

> *Those that are averse to constructive criticism aren't worth your time.*

sort of constructive criticism about myself, the office, or any team member, regardless of whether I find it was warranted, I thank that patient. Because for me, that shows the patient cares and wants my office to be a better place. In turn, I'll do everything I can to meet their needs and to make the office better.

Patients need doctors who create a forum for trust and transparency. It shouldn't be awkward at all when you give a doctor feedback as long as it's reasonable and the doctor can do something to improve. You have a right to make your doctor's office a better place and to tell your doctor when you see something that doesn't sit well with you or doesn't work for you.

GIVE YOUR DOCTOR THE CHANCE TO FIX IT.

If a patient comes to me, requests their records, and leaves the practice with no explanation, I suspect that patient may not be the best communicator. Some people aren't comfortable with the idea of confrontation. But I've even had distant relatives leave my practice without a single word and remain friends with me. We see each other at family functions and talk like nothing ever happened. It does make me wonder, though, *What was it that made you leave my practice?* If I had known, I would have tried to fix it. Sadly, by not telling me and giving me a chance, they lose the benefit of having a dentist friend that they have a direct line to for VIP care.

Even if you don't know your dentist personally, please give your dentist a chance to fix a problem. Remember, most dentists want to provide the best care for their patients, and we value our relationships with our patients and want to preserve those relationships.

BEWARE OF FALSE ASSUMPTIONS.

Giving your doctor a chance to fix something you don't like is better than the alternative, which is stewing over false assumptions. I've had patients who don't like to wait become angrier and angrier thinking that I've overbooked my appointments or, even worse, I choose to disrespect them and do not care if they have to wait. Rather than communicating that dislike and giving me a chance to fix the problem, those patients lose out by not speaking up. I've never intentionally booked more patients on my schedule than I know I can handle, but as I mentioned previously, emergencies and "spit" happens.

We only have so many spots on our daily schedule, and even with the extra fifteen minutes we allot for procedures, we never know if something outside of the norm will go wrong, like someone having trouble getting numb or their filling turning into a crown once we are in the midst of treatment. But none of that matters to the waiting patient. The day I stopped making excuses for running late was a much better day for me in terms of managing time. Patients perceive excuses as well-planned lies. What patients do care about is that I let them know if I'm running late, that I apologize for my tardiness, and that I give them options (no-wait appointments or even the opportunity to reschedule). To take it up a notch, we routinely give patients movie tickets as a goodwill gesture to demonstrate how much we value their time and appreciate their patience if we are running way behind schedule.

I once knew a doctor who, whenever he was running late in his office and a patient gave him a hard time, he would ask the upset waiting patient, "Have you ever been to the Cheesecake Factory?" Most people from South Florida have been to the Cheesecake Factory, so inevitably they answer yes, to which he would ask in response, "Do you wait in line for a table at the Cheesecake Factory?" Again, they would say *yes* because that place always has a wait. He would snap, "Well if you're gonna wait in line for the Cheesecake Factory, then you're gonna wait in line for me. Because what I'm doing is a lot more important than serving you a piece of Oreo cheesecake."

That is the quintessential poor example of a modern practice with patient-centered care in my opinion. That story might be humorous, but that doctor broke all the rules about managing your patients with kindness. That's why it's really important for you, the patient, to understand what happens behind the scenes in dentistry and, by extension, most healthcare provider's offices. What's going on is rarely something you are privy to as a patient, and although some of you demand to know why your doctor is running behind schedule, it does not change anything.

The trusting doctor–patient relationship is all about communication, and it's a two-way street. Patients need to ask about their treatments, and tell their doctors what they want, need, like, and dislike. It's imperative that the doctors receive that feedback and communicate to the patients what goes on behind the scenes whenever applicable.

BY THE WAY, DO YOUR REVIEWS LOOK THIS GOOD OR BETTER? IF NOT, WHY NOT?

My dental hygienist is fantastic. She explains everything, and is thoughtful. She even asks about my family! Marlene is so patient with me and helps with all of my insurance questions and payment options. And Dr. Mars is wonderful; he takes the time with his patients and makes each of them feel like they are the only ones in the office! Love the staff here! Couldn't ask for a better dental experience.
Erica F.

I've been going to Dental Care Group Aventura for over twenty years. Their staff is always professional, caring, and courteous. And Dr. Rick

Mars has a great sense of humor; he makes all his patients feel comfortable. Every three months I have my teeth cleaned with Cheryl, and Rick always pops in to do a quick check-up! Thank you again.
Elaine A.

This group of dentists are extremely worthy of an A rating. I've been a client for a number of years and have had different kinds of work on my teeth over the years. Never have I had an issue with any type of procedure. If anything, I've received the best in preventive care as well as corrective procedures. My teeth look great as a result. Dr. Mars took excellent care of me for over fourteen years after I moved to Miami. He always proved to be available for me whenever I had an emergency issue. My hygienist, Bonnie, was also awesome—extremely knowledgeable and competent in keeping my gums healthy. The treatment coordinator, Marlene, is also an excellent aspect of the office. Dental Care Group is by far the best in Aventura.
Marsha F.

I have been going to Dental Care Group Aventura for years. Dr. Mars and Claudia are the best! They care and demonstrate a high level of expertise. I would highly recommend them for the best dental care ever.
Lynne M.

Dr. Mars is amazing! He makes me feel comfortable at every appointment and my Invisalign process started and ended quickly.
Ariana H.

I have been seeing Dr. Mars and his team since 2003—sixteen years! I come regularly for cleanings; I have had fillings, root canals, and porcelain veneers on my top and bottom teeth. You name it, I have had it done. Dr. Mars and his entire staff between the office and dental assistants are the absolute best! Everyone is super professional, friendly, and very caring in regard to your comfort and your overall experience. In addition to a great, clean, and friendly environment, Dr. Mars is also somewhat of a comedian! He always has the funniest things to say or some quick little joke to make you laugh. The front office staff always gives you a nice warm welcome. They make you feel right a home. The Dental Care Group is a must when considering dental care. I would not dream of having another dentist or staff work on my teeth. They always have my best interest at heart. Thank you, Dr. Mars, and the entire staff for sixteen years of excellent service!

Andy B.

I've been going to Dr. Mars and Claudia for years. They have the most up-to-date practices and can do anything. They are the best! I wouldn't go anywhere else!

Judi D.

Dr. Rick Mars is absolutely incredible along with his staff. They are all so kind and look out for the needs of their patients. Having crooked teeth was always a big insecurity and now, thanks to Dr. Mars, I have a beautiful smile. He took the time to fix issues along the way and made sure I was happy with the end result. I highly recommend him.

Anna R.

In our next chapter, we'll talk about how to take that two-way communication even further as you learn about the importance of "educating" your doctor and being a warm receptor when they educate you.

Chapter 7

Good, Better, and Great Expectations

In this chapter, we'll talk about all of the good, better, and great things you should expect from your dental care providers. I'll also take the opportunity to address some common misconceptions you might have about what goes on behind the scenes in a modern dental practice. My goal once again is to educate you, the patient, the best I can so that you have the best possible experience with your healthcare provider.

HAVE GREAT BIG EXPECTATIONS.

You absolutely have every right to expect a high level of care when you visit your dentist. As I previously mentioned, I love when someone walks into our office and says, "I've never been to a dental office like this before. You guys are so thorough, you have advanced technology, and you are so personal!" All of the little and big things we do raise the expectations our patients have, and that's great!

What's a little trickier for us are the patients who have very low expectations. These patients usually have had bad experiences with their previous dentists and are a little jaded with the entire dental profession. This makes their next dentist feel a little bit like they are just a "rebound dentist" (just like that rebound boyfriend/girlfriend) until that patient can recover and go somewhere else when they are in a better state of mind.

It's usually not fun being "the rebound dentist." If you leave or break up with your previous dentist because of a terrible experience due to bad dentistry, financial conflict, personality conflict, office cleanliness issues, or appointment problems, you'll probably walk into your new dentist's office expecting the worst, which really isn't fair.

Every dental office is different. If what you previously experienced was negative, that doesn't mean your new experience will be either good or bad. It's up to you to go in thinking positive with high expectations and an open mind. You wouldn't stop dating if you went on one bad date. In the same sense, just because you had a bad experience with your previous dentist doesn't mean that you are doomed to another horrible experience. When you walk into a new dentist's practice, look for the good things before you notice the bad.

EXPECT MORE THAN "JUST HAVING YOUR TEETH CLEANED."

Being the rebound dentist can also be a tough act to follow, especially if the previous dentist wasn't doing the right thing. Those patients go from "just having their teeth cleaned" to proper dental care and wind up shocked by the amount of work they may need to correct what has (or hasn't) been done by their previous dentist. We must go the extra mile to educate these patients because of the "baggage" they often bring to our practices.

Erika, a new patient, came into my office. She was used to going to a dentist that cleaned her teeth every single visit, no matter what. On her first visit she said to me, "I was told I could get my teeth cleaned today." My office will always tell a new patient that we will not perform a cleaning on the first visit. That is because we take the time to do a thorough exam and take radiographs on every new patient examination. From there, we can recommend the type of hygiene procedure a patient needs for the next visit.

Instead of getting into a confrontation about who said what on the phone, knowing full well that Erika was being less than honest (she was totally lying), I responded, "Erika, you haven't been to the dentist in three years. You have multiple dental issues that we will discuss. More importantly, as far as getting your teeth cleaned, you'll need more than just a cleaning. Your periodontal exam shows that you require additional procedures to get your gums healthy." I bend over backward to educate Erika and show her how crucial it is that she have more than just a cleaning. I explain to her that a normal cleaning is a preventative treatment, but she requires a therapeutic treatment to properly address her periodontal needs because the damage has already been done.

More often than not, patients like Erika will protest, thinking I am trying to upsell her. But I take the time to explain further, "Erika, if you go to some place that just cleans your teeth, somewhere down the road, gum disease will rear its ugly head." After I explained the consequences of not doing the treatment, she had a change of heart and fortunately made a good decision. As the rebound dentist in this scenario, I really didn't want to be right about the consequences, but periodontal disease is progressive and never repairs itself. The last thing I ever want to say to a patient like Erika is "I told you so." Doing the right thing isn't a question of who's right or wrong; it's what every dentist should do and what every patient should allow their dentist to do.

If you have the wrong expectations or set the bar too low, you might not understand that the rebound dentist is trying to realign and reeducate you back to optimum dental health. Dentists routinely meet patients who say, "You're a dentist. That's great. I need a cleaning." No one (to date) ever says, "You're a dentist. That's great. I need a full evaluation of my oral health. I hope you can accommodate my request." We wish we would hear the latter more than the former. It would do wonders for the doctor–patient relationship, already strained by unscrupulous dentists.

YOU EXPECT YOUR DENTIST TO BE ON TIME, BUT WE EXPECT YOU TO BE ON TIME.

If you expect your doctor to be on time, you really should be on time. We give a fifteen-minute courtesy in our office to our patients if they are delayed, but we draw the line at fifteen minutes. Any more than that and the next patient has to wait and then the next, and the whole day just snowballs from there. Therefore, don't be upset if the front office has to say, "No, we're sorry. We need to reschedule you."

Some patients think, "I waited for my doctor last time, so my doctor should wait for me." But this situation is unfortunately not reciprocal. Patients wait for their dentist because there was likely a dental emergency or an issue with other patients being late. If this sounds like a double-edged sword, that's because it is. Doctors owe it to their patients to do everything in their power to run on time, but they do sometimes run behind for various reasons beyond the doctor's control. Patients should always arrive on time. If all of our patients made us wait, it would negatively impact all of our other patients that day and the entire office (our lifestyles and families). *It's absolutely imperative that patients respect their healthcare provider's time.* On that same note, if you are a person who is always early, and you show up thirty minutes early for your doctor and have to wait for ten minutes, don't hold your dentist accountable for your overly aggressive timeliness. I know it sounds crazy, but we recently had a patient upset that she waited forty minutes when in fact we were just minutes behind schedule. Welcome to our world!

EXPECT TO PARTICIPATE IN YOUR OWN DENTAL HEALTH.

Most dentists are fairly intelligent people, or else they wouldn't be dentists. It's fairly simple to deduce when a patient isn't doing the right thing when it comes to taking care of their teeth. When patients commit to wearing their Invisalign aligners, their teeth get straighter. When they floss every day, their gums generally will not bleed. It's really very straightforward, and there are few exceptions. We can see evidence of action or inaction right there in a patient's mouth. Way too often patients are looking for someone to blame, and most of the time that someone should be the person that they see in the mirror. Flossing is a classic example of this. News flash! We know very few of you floss on a daily basis and many of you floss only the night before your dental appointment. There is an old dental joke that goes like this:

Dentist: When was the last time you flossed?

Patient: You should know, you were there!

So when your dentist tells you your gums are bleeding and you require a deep scaling, additional treatment, or even a trip to the periodontist,

> *Way too often patients are looking for someone to blame, and most of the time that someone should be the person that they see in the mirror.*

don't ask why if you haven't seen dental floss in six months. Got it?

When patients don't assume any responsibility for the consequences of their actions (or inactions), it puts a strain on the doctor–patient relationship. The dentist is automatically put in the position of having to struggle with the patient to get them to do the right thing, rather than work with them to keep them healthy. The best policy for patients is to accept responsibility for their role in their own dental health. By doing this, they strengthen the doctor–patient relationship because it becomes a team effort rather than an adversarial one.

EXPECT TO ASK QUESTIONS AND GET ANSWERS.

We go more into you educating yourself and being educated in chapter 8, but for this chapter, I do want to address this briefly. The last thing I always ask my patients after I present their treatment plan to them is "Do you have any questions?" At this point, it's important for you, the patient, to ask questions. One of those questions should always be "What are the consequences if I don't do the treatment, and what are the benefits if I do the treatment?"

I enjoy educating patients. I get fulfillment from patients asking me multiple questions like "How long is my treatment going to take? What are some of the side effects for the treatment? How much discomfort is involved with the treatment?" I want patients to ask as many questions as they can think of so I can provide them with as many answers as I possibly can. This kind of communication, when everybody understands what's going on, mitigates potential conflict down the road.

Education helps you get the greatest value from your treatment. You need to understand the problem, the consequences, and the solution for your treatment so you can be informed about your health.

DON'T EXPECT US TO ASK THE AWKWARD QUESTION.

When doctors discuss consequences, they should try to cover every possible outcome from doing or not doing a treatment. There's only one outcome that most healthcare providers won't voluntarily discuss, which is what happens if you, the patient, cancel the treatment after scheduling or while in the middle of treatment. This awkward subject exists in a category of its own and doesn't fall under medical consequences because it's on you, the patient, to bring it up. We won't because it portrays a lack of trust. We don't anticipate patients not coming through for themselves because we trust they are there to get help and will follow through with the treatment until it's done.

Think of it this way: my patients don't anticipate that I will start their procedures and suddenly decide I need to keep a prior engagement halfway through, leaving them in the operatory. In the same sense, healthcare providers don't expect that you will quit treatment once it's underway (which is at the time of scheduling). That's why it's important that you, the patient, ask your dentist that awkward question, "What happens if I cancel?" and hold yourself accountable if you do back out of your treatment.

If you schedule treatment, start it, and suddenly have to stop for whatever reason, then the chips will land in a way no one wanted them to. Discontinuing treatment or noncompliance negates quality care. The negative consequences impact your health and possibly your finances. That's because in our office, as soon as a patient schedules treatment, we immediately research what we need and incur the expense of ordering supplies and scheduling staff for the treatment.

Bring up the awkward question if you need to, but don't hold your healthcare provider responsible for not bringing it up. If you understand this, it really helps the doctor–patient relationship. In all fairness, I understand that this question is comparable to not discussing divorce when you get married, and when it happens, the split will not always be smooth. But if you know you are the type of person that may not see things through to the very end, it is imperative that you inquire as to the consequences.

DON'T EXPECT X-RAYS TO KILL YOU.

A patient I've known since grade school was in my office recently with the hygienist. The hygienist pulled me aside and said, "Dr. Mars, Brian is refusing to have X-rays." Generally, when a patient refuses to have X-rays, it's due to a financial issue or concern about radiation.

Since X-rays are usually covered by insurance, most often a refusal to take radiographs is a concern about radiation. This happened to be the case with Brian. I said to Brian, "Brian, permit me to explain to you the facts about X-rays in the dental office." We discussed that most people don't know that they are exposed to more radiation flying on an airplane or walking down the street than the amount they get from a few X-rays in a dental office. I gave Brian a clearer understanding, and like most patients once they are educated, he consented to having his radiographs taken.

The bottom line is, by educating patients like Brian, I am fulfilling his expectation for proper care, starting with giving him the correct diagnosis by way of radiographs. My job as a doctor is to help align my patients' expectations with my goal to provide great care. Patients have a right to great dentistry. You can expect your dentist to do the right thing. If you come in with the negative or unrealistic expectations, it's your dentist's duty to realign those negative or unrealistic expectations through education so that you don't get in the way of your own good health.

EXPECT THAT EVEN DOCTORS HAVE BAD DAYS.

As I write this book, I realize that portions of the book are actually a disclaimer for past or future events, hopefully not just for me, but for every dentist that reads this book. The ending of this chapter is the perfect example.

Even on one of my worst days ever, when my schedule was running behind and patients were getting angry, I went with the flow, and it all turned out for the best. I remember a day that I felt like I once again was being tested by God. One of my team members came to me and told me her father had pancreatic cancer, which unfortunately, is how

I lost my mother, so it really hit home. Not fifteen seconds later (no exaggeration), while I was still standing in the same spot, stunned, another team member basically fell in my arms sobbing that her father was dying right then in hospice. She had to leave the office to be with him.

Some of you might think it is not worth saying, but I want to leave you with the knowledge that your doctors have good days and bad days just like you.

Thank the Lord my office doesn't have days like that often. Here's my point: even after hearing such horrible news, I couldn't bring the sadness I was feeling for my team members to any patient I saw in my chair that morning. For the next three hours, I was happy-go-lucky Dr. Rick Mars and did great dentistry with a smile on my face. I was very pleasant and professional with my patients. None of them would have guessed that my heart was broken. I sucked it up at a level that I didn't even think was possible.

Some of you might think it is not worth saying, but I want to leave you with the knowledge that your doctors have good days and bad days just like you. But we have to remain professional and do our best work because your health is of the utmost importance, but we are humans too. All that we ask is that you be understanding with us, just like you expect us to be understanding with you, as there will be days that won't be your dentist's best days. Bottom line: Some days we need to cut each other a break, and that can only strengthen our doctor–patient relationship.

Now that we've talked about all the expectations you can have as a patient in your dental care provider's office, we'll talk more on a subject we've only touched upon: how you can get the most out of your investment into your healthy mouth.

Chapter 8

How to Be a Good Patient

This chapter explains how to be a good patient, not only so you make your dentist's life easier but most importantly so you get the best quality care. I want you to get the most from your investment into your mouth. You can do that through education. Good patients are educated: they educate themselves, they listen as their doctors educate them, and they in turn educate their doctors. That's right. Patients can actually educate their doctors. Educated patients understand why it's important to put their money where their mouth is!

WHAT'S THE PLAN?

In 2015, the Canadian Broadcast Corporation (CBC) did a hidden camera investigation called "Is Your Dentist Ripping You Off?" The reporter had a baseline exam conducted on herself at the University of Toronto Dental School, then set off with her radiographs to get several other opinions for her treatment. The results varied from the university exam widely, so the reporter concluded that every other dentist was trying to scam her. Any patient who saw the exposé would be convinced that the reporter clearly made her case: dentists are greedy con artists, and we shouldn't trust the lot of them. The reporter implied that we all should go to the dental school to get the most honest and accurate treatment. But the exposé was flawed from the very beginning.

Dental schools are great for teaching the same tried-and-true methods that have been used for decades. It cannot be said that dental schools are the gold standard for modern dentistry. I mean no offense by this, as they often lead in dental research. But who's to say that the University of Toronto Dental School is the absolute authority on dentistry?

The reporter, in my opinion, really just exposed a problem we have in modern dentistry—communication. Many dentists do not do a good enough job of educating and thus communicating with their patients, and most patients don't do a good enough job educating themselves.

We have a saying in dentistry that if you put ten dentists in a room with a single patient, they will come up with ten different treatment plans. This is exactly what happened with the CBC investigation. What this saying really means is that there's more than one way to skin a cat. Okay, that's another saying, so let me explain. If a patient reports to a dental office with a missing tooth, one dentist will suggest an implant, another dentist might say to do a bridge, and yet a third might recommend replacing the tooth with something removable, such as a partial denture. The point is, all of those treatment plans are objectively correct. The great thing about dentistry is the multitude of creative solutions available to patients. Your dental provider will give you the plan that he or she thinks is the best for you, but you need to ask the right questions to make sure you understand the treatment options.

The great thing about dentistry is the multitude of creative solutions available to patients.

HOW TO GET AN HONEST SECOND OPINION.

In this book I've written many times about trust and education and how important both are. But sometimes, even though you trust your dentist, you might hear a treatment plan that just doesn't sit well with you. This is a good indicator that you need further education by your current dentist, another treatment option by your current dentist, or a second opinion by another dentist. We have a handout in our office that instructs patients on how to get an honest second opinion. Here are some tips that we share on that handout:

1. Get a copy of your radiographs from your current dentist to take to your second opinion dentist.

2. Present your radiographs to the second dentist, and let them examine your mouth. If they pry you for information about your first opinion just say, "I'd like to hear your opinion please."

3. Never show the second dentist your treatment plan until they give their final suggestions. Some unscrupulous dentists, after evaluating your original diagnosis, will offer less treatment because they want to compete for your business. Give that second dentist an opportunity to creatively come up with an unbiased answer based on what they think is best.

4. If they prescribe a treatment plan that's in line with the one you have, wonderful. You have now confirmed that your dentist was presenting a correct treatment, and barring unforeseen circumstances, you should be comfortable proceeding with your dentist.

5. If the second dentist's plan is very different, you should then provide them with a copy of your treatment plan and ask, "Why do you think yours is the best approach as opposed to what my dentist told me?"

6. Listen carefully to the second dentist's explanation. Get a copy of that second dentist's treatment plan, and be sure to go back to your dentist. Say to your dentist, "I went for a second opinion. This is what I was told." Then ask, "Why do you feel your approach is better?"

By following these steps, you will get the best second opinion in the world. This approach requires both dentists to thoroughly think through your case and provide you with all of the necessary information. Now you can make an educated decision about your treatment based on the best course of action for your health and wellness. That is the primary factor one should use when making decisions about one's healthcare. I know it is easy to say, but now it is up to the patient to figure out how to pay for the best care.

EDUCATE YOURSELF TO ADVOCATE FOR YOUR HEALTH.

I mentioned taking an active role in your health by getting educated about your body in chapter 7, but I'll go into more detail here. When it comes to your health, what you don't know will indeed hurt you. The worst thing that can happen is that you don't get the treatment you need and something disastrous happens. The second worst thing that can happen is that you do get treatment, but you didn't actually need it.

Taking an active role means you not only do your own research and get a second opinion but you also listen carefully to your doctor when your doctor educates you. I call this being a *warm receptor*. Sometimes, I will educate a patient and just lose them. If my patient's attention wanders or they look uninterested, I try to shock them a little bit. Usually I just stop talking. That really gets their attention! If that doesn't work, there is sadly nothing more I can do. The onus is on that patient, but I'd rather it not be.

I go to work to make a living, but the last thing I want to hear is that I missed something on a patient. Or God forbid, I miss something that costs somebody their life! That is every doctor's worst nightmare. Recently a family friend was in another office, and their dentist failed to premedicate the patient who recently had hip replacement surgery. Bacterial endocarditis ensued, and it resulted in a long hospitalization and a cascade of terrible medical issues. It was terrible that this oversight nearly cost a person their life. My job is to educate my patients because their health depends on it. Sometimes I have to do it over and over because patients don't want to hear it. I'll write this again because it is so vital to your health:

Your job as a patient is to be a warm receptor for the education the doctor gives you. Failing to be a warm receptor (for whatever reason) can have disastrous results.

Doctors can educate you all day long, but if you don't buy into what we tell you, it's time for you to do some research and verify the information. Sometimes the information is just a little shocking—for example, when we tell patients about the correlation between periodontal disease and heart disease or stroke—that's a hard pill to swallow for a lot of people because they have never heard of this correlation before.

Other times we haven't yet established trust with that patient. If a patient comes to our office through a referral from a friend or family member, we have a level of credibility with that patient and thus a level of trust. But if a patient

Your job as a patient is to be a warm receptor for the education the doctor gives you.

is new to our office, for example they picked us out of an insurance book, they might be a bit taken aback by the amount of information we provide them. For a lot of patients, it's brain overload.

But at the same time, you as a patient need to insist on understanding what you're hearing. Ask the right questions back. Do some research online. Unfortunately some dentists resort to scare tactics by threatening dire consequences, for instance, "If you don't get this cavity filled today, you're going to need a root canal tomorrow!" That's extremely unlikely because cavities don't grow that fast. But you wouldn't know that unless you did some research or asked more questions. Most of the time, dentists are very honest and straightforward in how they deal with their patients. You have to be a warm receptor and receive that information with the appropriate amount of attention and respect.

KNOW WHY YOU NEED TREATMENT.

As I previously alluded to, for some reason, many people perceive that dentistry is elective. That is so far from the truth. Sadly most people just don't realize the consequences of poor dental health. Ask the average person, What's the worst thing that can happen if you have poor dental health? I think most people would answer, "I'd lose my teeth." Very few people would answer, "I could potentially lose my life." Don't misunderstand my point here, as I believe losing one's teeth should be reason enough to motivate a patient, but potential life and death has got to seal the deal! Patients will routinely spend over $100 per week on hair and nails, but oftentimes will not make a similar investment in their oral health, even if they have the financial resources. Every dentist's job is to create value so their patients will prioritize their oral health.

Imagine if you lose all of your teeth or if you have rampant gum disease in your mouth. Not a pretty picture. Now imagine that it potentially could cut your life short! I've had family members with poor periodontal health who have had heart attacks. I met a young woman—forty-six years old—who had a major stroke. She wasn't my patient, but her husband called me and asked if I could come over on a Sunday to examine her. You see, she was in a wheelchair and couldn't leave the house. She was only just starting therapy as a result of the stroke. I examined her and saw severe periodontal disease and tremendous plaque buildup. It made me so sad. I wished she would have walked in my office years ago. I was sure that I could have made a difference in her life and quite possibly I could have prevented her from having the stroke. I would have examined her and seen the plaque buildup. Then I would have immediately done a saliva test for C-reactive protein. If that test came up as positive, I would have advised her to see a doctor immediately or called her healthcare provider myself, as the presence of C-reactive protein in saliva indicates a high risk for stroke, diabetes, heart disease, or hypertension. I also would have taken her blood pressure, as we do with all of our patients, and quite possibly disaster might have been averted.

Several years ago, I saw a patient who was a personal trainer that reported to the office for a consultation concerning his periodontal disease. He had a tremendous amount of plaque buildup. I shared my diagnosis with him, explained the treatment, and most importantly, educated him on the possible outcome of not doing the treatment, citing the studies that connect plaque buildup with stroke. He said that he didn't have the money for treatment and left my office. Much to my dismay, I found out two years later that he had a major stroke. While I can't 100 percent pinpoint a single cause for his stroke, I will tell you that this trainer was built like an Adonis and was in the peak of health. If you saw him without a shirt on, he looked like the cover of *Men's Fitness* magazine. The only place I could see on his body that wasn't in the best shape was his mouth.

Those are two very different stories of patients who were not educated about the importance of dental health in a timely manner and saw the same terrible end result. Modern dentists are not "drill, fill, and bill" when it comes to your health. We take our responsibility to educate you seriously. If we can save lives, we're going to save lives. Please be a warm receptor … it could save your life.

KNOW WHY YOU DON'T NEED TREATMENT.

As I mentioned previously, the last question we always ask patients is "Do you have any questions about the treatment?" We give the patient multiple opportunities to ask because we want to be sure they are educated. At the end of the day, knowledge is power. If your doctor has educated you and you've done the research, but you feel something isn't essential to your treatment, then ask about it. Don't rule out the possibility that you haven't been educated enough.

The last question you ever want to ask your dentist is "Why did you pull my tooth out? Wasn't it perfectly fine?" That is a question you want to ask *before* your dentist pulls your tooth out. Countless times in my career, I have had patients who have said, "I had all this dental work done when I was younger, and I am sure I didn't need to have that work done." I then think to myself, *Wow. That's terrible*. You've got to be very sure when somebody's performing a physical procedure on you that you completely understand why that procedure is being performed.

> *If your doctor has educated you and you've done the research, but you feel something isn't essential to your treatment, then ask about it.*

Sy Syms, the founder and chairman of the Syms retail apparel chain, used to say, "An educated consumer is our best customer." I can use that and say, "An educated patient is our best patient." I want everybody to understand why I prescribe treatments. I never want anybody coming back to me after their treatment second-guessing why they had it done. Ask all those questions before your treatment is started. On his first visit to my office, Jacob informed my hygienist that he chose our office because of the overwhelming numbers of positive reviews, but had concern over several negative reviews, which he admitted was all that he read. I thanked Jacob for being so candid and then explained that we do not censor negative reviews and explained the origin of each of these reviews. Jacob, now the truly educated patient, had his fears allayed with his concerns addressed. I was so impressed with his approach, I promised to put him in my book (promise kept).

EDUCATE YOUR DOCTOR.

Because we live in the information age, patients are sometimes exposed to new advances or techniques that we haven't yet explored. With so many different devices out there, it's difficult for doctors to pick up on every single new gadget on the market. We might hear a mention of something new in a dental journal or see it at a trade show, but if none of our colleagues are talking about it, we lack firsthand experience to know whether it's a good investment. This is the patient's chance to educate their doctors.

As I mentioned earlier, many years ago, I had a patient ask me about a new device called the Wand. Her previous dentist used it to relieve the discomfort of injections, which is often the most fearful part of a dental procedure. Plain and simple, with the dental meetings and seminars I attend and the countless dental journals I read, my patient schooled me on the latest technology for comfortable injections. Without my patient educating me, I wouldn't have brought the device into my practice over fifteen years ago when it first came on the market.

If you see something new that will make your experience better and more comfortable, it's up to you to educate your doctor. Not a thing wrong with that!

ASK TO SEE THE RESULTS OF YOUR INVESTMENT.

As with any service or product you purchase, you want to see the results of that investment. Dentistry is no different. Even if the procedure isn't cosmetic, it's smart to ask your dentist to show you the results of the treatment.

In this chapter, we talked about the importance of education before and during your treatment. Here is your opportunity to continue your education after treatment too. Rather than limit your evaluation of your dentist to time, cost, or customer service, think about your dental work like you consider mechanical work to your car. Sometimes you can't see all the work done under the hood, but you can ask the mechanic how the car should function now that it's fixed.

After treatment, dentists can and should show you radiographs of your teeth and point out how nice, for example, a crown margin appears. Or if it's a tough filling, they can radiograph or even photograph the filling to ensure everything is clinically acceptable and show you. I know I want my patients to see the great dentistry that I'm performing on them, and I'm sure your dentist does too.

If you're searching for an amazing modern dental practice in your area, my next chapter will really help you on that search. In it, I explain how to begin the hunt, what questions to ask, and the kinds of things you should expect and look out for!

Chapter 9

Vetting Your Dentist

A patient recently gave me a coffee mug that I now keep on my desk in my office. It says, "Don't confuse your Google search with my dental degree." It is a constant reminder of the time I had a patient in my chair who did exactly that. Ariela came in with a cracked tooth. (Sometimes this is tricky to diagnose, as cracks can happen internally and aren't visible to the naked eye or even with an X-ray.) I informed her of her problem, the consequences of not treating the problem, and offered my solution, which unfortunately was a removal of the cracked tooth and replacement with a dental implant. I also suggested she speak to my oral surgeon who was at my office that day for an immediate second opinion.

While awaiting the specialist, Ariela googled the phrase "cracked tooth" on her smartphone. After skimming the information, she decided that I was wrong about her treatment. She became very adamant that my treatment was too aggressive. I explained to her again that if her tooth weren't treated the way I suggested, she could end up with more problems down the road. My specialist came in and confirmed the diagnosis and my treatment plan. Ariela went home, still insisting that I wasn't giving her the best option and adamant that I send her for a very expensive root canal treatment that her Google search indicated was a viable option. Fortunately for her, she had a change of heart and came back to have the proposed treatment, not "Google's treatment." Don't get me wrong, I *love* Google and use it almost daily, but always consider the source and know the World Wide Web is full of misinformation.

While I could have gotten defensive, I didn't. This kind of thing happens all the time in dentistry (thus, the coffee mug). I was more worried about whether she would get the treatment she needed rather than bruise my ego. The lesson here is this: the internet has changed the world by providing limitless information at our fingertips, but it's often a very poor substitute for the wisdom and expertise we have right in front of our eyes.

DO YOUR HOMEWORK BEFORE YOU SEE YOUR DOCTOR.

That's not to say the internet is a bad thing. It can be very helpful when you're vetting a new dentist. Good patients always do a little research before they see a new doctor rather than just picking a random one off a provider list from their insurance companies. This doesn't necessarily mean you should read every online review and take it for gospel. You should of course talk to your friends. Then talk to your other medical professionals. Better yet, talk to any friends that happen to be medical professionals.

When I'm looking for a new healthcare provider, I tend to start with referrals from friends that are also doctors. Marketing isn't as important to my own practice as word of mouth. We ask our patients for referrals, either online or off, as this is the sincerest source of patient-to-patient information exchange. One kind of referral is online patient testimonials, which often provide firsthand, credible information about a dentist or a dental practice. I did a veneer case on Brody, which was four days before his wedding. We did a big reveal and took a video of him looking at himself in the mirror. You would think he was a paid actor. He and his fiancée were stunned. All they could say was "Oh my God!" This is why I show up to work. I have to make a living, of course, but patient satisfaction and testimonials like that make it worth my while. We put the video on all of our social media (Instagram, Facebook, and Twitter). When the world sees a real experience like that, it's deeply meaningful and genuine. It's priceless!

READ ONLINE REVIEWS WITH A CRITICAL EYE.

Be sure that you take everything you read online with a grain of salt. Some review sites, such as Yelp, reportedly withhold positive reviews until they receive a subscription fee to their service from the business being reviewed. Some review sites won't remove negative reviews even if the business can prove their inauthenticity or malicious intent from the author, even if it is a competitor. Patients don't know how businesses struggle with these online reviews, which can be a death knell for a doctor with a newly established practice.

My wife was at the cardiologist's the other day with her parents. The doctor was running three and a half hours late. His receptionist explained to my wife that earlier that day, a patient had had a heart attack right in the reception area. He saved the patient's life! Of course he was running late because he did an amazing thing. Who would not forgive a doctor for doing that? Can you imagine if a patient gave him a negative review that day, especially without all of the facts?

In today's world, patients wield power like they never previously had, which can be a good or bad thing depending on the patient. Some patients threaten their healthcare providers with this power. I recently had a patient threaten to write a bad review because she did not "like the look on my face." (Admittedly, I might have fueled the fire when I responded that this is the only look I have.) Patients can and will write reviews online that devastate their doctors. If they write a bad review, healthcare providers are unable to defend themselves because it's a violation of the Health Insurance Portability and Accountability Act (HIPAA) of 1996, which protects patients' privacy.

Recently I referred a patient's son, Sandy, to my oral surgeon. For the first time in my career, a patient balked. She said, "We have some hesitations." When I asked her why, her answer was that my surgeon had a few negative reviews. I was flabbergasted because he's an excellent oral surgeon. He's worked on thousands of my patients, including my own children. While the mom was still in my office, I went online with her to see my surgeon's reviews. He had some excellent reviews, but he also had two not-so-good reviews. I quickly discovered that she didn't understand enough about what goes on behind the scenes in a dental practice and thus couldn't look at the reviews critically.

My surgeon had only two complaints written about him. The first was that he's only available part time in a few different offices. The reviewer saw that as a negative, failing to realize that many specialists work in several different offices, as single practices rarely require enough niche services to warrant full-time hours. I explained to her that if there were an emergency with her son, my surgeon is always on call to help. Additionally, our practice is open six days a week, and all of our doctors are capable of covering each other's emergencies. The second negative review was about how the doctor had a tremendously long wait time. The reviewer waited an hour and a half and was very upset. It mentioned that my surgeon actually had a complicated procedure immediately before the reviewer's appointment, but in spite of that, the reviewer was very unforgiving.

Fortunately my patient was direct enough to point out the negative reviews and open enough to walk through them with me so I could explain on my surgeon's behalf. By the way, Sandy had an amazing experience with my oral surgeon! Following her son's treatment, she volunteered to write a positive review, which we gladly accepted.

Think about it: how many reviews have you personally written and why? In general, people who bother to write reviews are disgruntled and want recourse and even "revenge." Businesses need to provide something exceptional for somebody to take the time to write a positive review. If you go to the dentist and you're seen on time, the doctor numbs you up sufficiently, the doctor does your filling, it's a pain-free procedure, and you walk out, then everything happens as expected. Rarely would any patient take the time to write a glowing review about that experience unless requested to do so. But if there is any issue, watch out! Many people in the world today feel that their sole purpose in life is to inform the world via online reviews of their negative experiences. I wish they had the same burning desire to let the world know about their positive experiences.

INTERVIEW YOUR DOCTOR AND THEIR TEAM.

Like many modern dental practices, I mentioned that in our office, we offer a tour of our practice to potential patients so they can meet the team and see how we work. If any of my patients want to just sit down and talk to me before their regular appointments, I'm always willing and open. Parents interview pediatricians for their children; it makes sense that people would want to interview a potential dentist or even their current one.

"What is your level of experience?" is a great question to ask if you're interviewing a potential healthcare provider. Every doctor has to start somewhere, so there's a chance that doctor might not have much experience at all. When was the last time you asked your dentist where they went to dental school? Or how many years they've been practicing? Some of the best clinical dentists in the world didn't go to the top dental schools, but if not, the important question is, What makes them top clinical dentists right now?

> *Don't make assumptions;*
> *just ask questions.*

You can ask them how many times they've done a certain procedure and even ask to see photos of their cases. I can't even tell you the number of crowns I've done in my life. Maybe I can. Let me do the math: I've averaged approximately twenty crowns a week throughout my career. That's over a thousand crowns a year. I've been practicing for thirty years. That's over thirty thousand crowns! That number implies that I'm very comfortable with this type of procedure. But here's a scary thought: somebody out there was my first crown. Somebody else was my second. On a positive note, my 30,001st case certainly went smoother than my first or second. Bottom line: Become informed and don't be afraid to ask the critical questions of your dentist.

All joking aside, just because a dentist looks young doesn't mean he or she doesn't have experience with a certain procedure. On the other hand, just because a dentist looks older doesn't mean he or she is experienced with a procedure. Don't make assumptions; *just ask questions.* You deserve honest answers so you can make educated decisions.

FIND OUT WHY THEY CHARGE WHAT THEY CHARGE.

A big part of my practice is Invisalign. So many times, patients come to me and say, "I heard there's a dentist who does Invisalign for substantially less than you do on Groupon." It amazes me that anyone would go to a dentist that offers rock-bottom prices and not stop and wonder how they can afford to do that. The answer is, like anything else in this world, you often get what you pay for.

Sometimes those dentists are actually losing money. An educated patient would walk into that office and ask that doctor how many Invisalign cases they have done. The chances are very good the number will be very low. They might even be offering a less expensive clear aligner therapy and falsely calling it Invisalign. Be wary because top doctors would never offer their expertise for rock-bottom prices.

I talked to my friend Bunnie the other day, who lives on the West Coast. She said her general dentist casually offered to treat her daughter with Invisalign and even quoted a very discounted price. At first, Bunnie was excited. Then she grew suspicious when the dentist said the treatment would only take a year without even taking a mold or doing a scan of her daughter. She told me, "I just kind of looked at him and said, 'Okay, we'll let you know.'" Then she went and did some research, asking other parents whom they used and reading reviews online. She found a highly recommended specialist in her same city. She interviewed her, was impressed, and ended up using her even though she charged twice as much! My friend said, "Dr. Mars, if I'm going to have this done, it needs to be done right because she is my daughter. She's fourteen and nervous enough. The last thing she needs is a bad experience!"

We hear these kinds of stories all the time in my profession. When you're vetting a dentist, these are the things that you need to look for. Do your research, and remember, when something sounds too good to be true, it almost definitely is!

EDUCATE YOURSELF ON YOUR DENTAL OFFICE'S SURROUNDINGS.

It's important for patients to look around their healthcare provider's office with a discerning eye. What can you measure as a patient? Is your doctor trying to impress you with fancy artwork and a $20,000 fish tank in the reception area? Or is it a simple, clean office with furniture that isn't worn out or stained?

Try the light bulb test the next time you go to the doctor. Are the light bulbs changed? That tells you a lot about the office that you're in. We have quarterly team meetings where everybody in the whole office gets together and discusses how we can make our office better. One meeting, I asked everybody to close their eyes. Then I asked, "Who can tell me if there are any burned-out light bulbs in this room right now and if so, how many?" It was amazing how many my staff noticed. I told them a funny thing: some patients might look up at those burned-out bulbs and think, *Wow, they can't even change a light bulb. What kind of office have I walked into?* Others wouldn't even notice. Regardless, as soon as a light bulb burns out, it's our job to immediately fix it because we don't know if the next patient who walks through our doors will be giving our office "the light bulb test." We're very proud of our facilities, and we want patients to make it their home. I might own the office with my partner, but our dental office really belongs to the patients.

Even without being a medical expert, you can size up the equipment your doctor uses. Do you often hear that they can't do something because they have a broken piece of equipment? Things break all the time, but how quickly do they get them fixed in your doctor's office? How new is the technology? This is an easy one. If the radiographic equipment looks like it's from the 1960s and the dental chairs haven't been changed since 1910, ask yourself where's the money going in that office. Why aren't they putting any of it back into the office to update it so it's comfortable for the patients?

Also find out about where they source their supplies. These are great questions you should ask your dentist: What lab do you use, and why do you use them? What implant system are you using? Where are your crowns manufactured? There are dentists that have been sending their dental work out of the country for many years only later to find out the materials used were not only inferior but toxic. Who makes your dental cements or composite filling materials? (You should recognize some of the more reputable names such as 3M and Fuji.)

Your dental office is your dental office. You want the right bells and whistles, but you don't want them to get out of hand, like that fish tank. I've had patients say to me, "My friend's dentist has 3-D glasses for patients to use while sitting in the chair" or "My neighbor's dentist has Netflix." We have televisions in every operatory because we want to keep the patients entertained. But at the same time we don't have those kinds of bells and whistles because who wants to hang out all day in the dentist's office? People want to get in and out. They're not coming in to spend the evening bingeing on Netflix in their 3-D glasses. The important thing is that your dentist's office is clean, updated, and comfortable for you and shows pride of ownership. Those are things you can see just by observing.

EDUCATE YOURSELF ON THE LESS OBVIOUS THINGS LIKE OFFICE CULTURE.

I like to put pictures of my family up in my office, and my team likes to do the same. I want patients to see my wife and my three kids that I'm very proud of and to know I'm a family guy. When a patient interviews me or as I'm interviewing a new patient, I always ask about the patient's family and readily answer any questions about mine. I want patients to know who I am, what I do, and what I stand for.

This is the culture in our entire office. We also believe in giving back to the community, which we think of as an extended family. We do a free day of dentistry every year called Dentistry from Our Hearts. This past year, we reached our goal of giving away a million dollars of free dentistry to the community, and we are going to keep going beyond that. We have pictures of that special day in our operatories, and we use them as screen savers on our computer screens. We put these things up to remind ourselves who we are. We also want our patients to know about our culture. We want to make the world a better place every single day. That's what we're striving to do. You should be able to learn about your healthcare provider's office culture by looking around the practice and by talking to members of the dental team.

DISCUSS WHEN IT'S TIME TO SEE A SPECIALIST.

Depending on where you live, it may not be easy to access a certain type of dental specialist, such as a periodontist, oral surgeon, or endodontist. If you live in a metropolitan area, specialists are as widespread as general dentists are. But in rural areas, specialists are rare to nonexistent. In that case, unless you're willing to travel, you will have to rely on general practitioners for all your healthcare needs. Something many patients don't know is that every general dentist is technically qualified to do anything a specialist does. For instance, a general dentist can do orthodontics, even Invisalign. General dentists are trained to perform oral surgery, root canals, and even gum surgery.

> *We want to make the world a better place every single day.*

For the majority of patients living in more populated areas, they might wonder when and if it's a good idea to see a specialist. In my practice, like many modern dental practices these days, we have all the specialists under one roof. The reason we do that is to provide the best care for our patients from the most qualified dental professional.

General dentists who are very proficient in a certain procedure, for example in root canals, make it their subspecialty. They will have done the extra training and have gained experience doing that procedure on patients. That being said, very few general dentists can claim that they are as capable or better at doing a certain procedure compared to a specialist in that niche. They know that a specialist, who does that particular procedure exclusively day in and day out, would do a better job than a general dentist.

Last year I was in Michigan checking into a hotel, and a young lady working the front desk noticed that I was a dentist and informed me she needed a root canal. I asked her who was doing her root canal, and she told me it was her general dentist. I asked her which tooth she was having the root canal on, and she pointed to her upper second molar. I asked, "Have you thought about seeing a specialist for that tooth? That tends to be a tough tooth." She said her dentist had never talked to her about seeing a specialist.

I educated her about how complex a root canal procedure on an upper second molar can be and suggested that she might want to go back and ask her dentist for a referral to a specialist. She asked me, "Do you think he is going to be offended?" I said that he should want the best quality care for her and I doubted he would be offended.

Even if there's a specialist who does a certain procedure in your area, it is not always necessary to see them. For example, I'm a general dentist, but I am also a provider of Invisalign. As you know from the introduction, I'm on Invisalign's Global Faculty (one of only six in this entire country) and a Master Faculty member (one of five general dentists in this country). I have achieved Invisalign Platinum Plus Provider status, and I was honored this year as the GP Faculty Member of the Year. When it comes to Invisalign, I provide the same level and, in some cases, an even higher level of expertise as most orthodontists. I've received the same training they have, and I teach nationally and globally to others in my profession.

A lot of my patients might get a second opinion from an orthodontist when it comes to Invisalign. Some orthodontists insist that orthodontists straighten teeth, not general dentists. There has been debate over the years between general dentists and orthodontists: Who should be performing Invisalign? About half the cases are performed by general dentists and half of them are performed by orthodontists. So far, that has been a winning formula for patients, dentists/orthodontists, and Invisalign.

Bottom line: For any procedure, if a general dentist has the experience level and the training and is comfortable in the modalities and most importantly knows their limitations, then that general dentist can perform most dental procedures with competence. A few times in my career, I have referred out Invisalign cases as orthodontic cases. I know my limitations, and I know Invisalign's limitations, and some patients are simply not good candidates for that procedure. That being said, over 95 percent of the cases that come my way are clearly Invisalign cases, and I'm very comfortable doing them as most general dentists are comfortable treating the cases that they accept in their offices.

The same can be said for a tooth extraction. Almost any general dentist can do a simple extraction, but if you had to have an impacted wisdom tooth removed, you should be in the hands of a qualified oral surgeon. The bottom line is to communicate with your dentist.

How do you, as the patient, know when a procedure should be done by a specialist or if it's something your general dentist can take care of? The answer is, you don't know unless you ask. Any time your doctor suggests a treatment, be sure you ask three fundamental questions:

1. How difficult is this procedure?
2. How many times have you done this procedure?
3. Is this something that I can see a specialist for, and is there any reason a specialist should not do the procedure?

Your doctor, whether a general practitioner or a specialist, should leave no room for doubt that you're in the right place. They should be able to readily give you multiple reasons why they are qualified to do a procedure. If you have any concerns, always get a second opinion.

If a patient questions my credentials or asks me about my experience, I will always answer in a sincere, educated way. I would never get offended about those kinds of questions, as I love an educated patient and I love to educate patients. Every dentist in a modern dental practice should feel the same way.

Warning Bells and Peace Signs

Please use this as a handy checklist that summarizes everything we talked about in this book.

CHECKLIST FOR DENTISTS: DO YOU HAVE A MODERN DENTAL PRACTICE?

Doctors, use your checklist as a test: Do you have a modern dental practice? It's okay if you can't check all the boxes right away—use it as an action list to do each thing one by one.

CHAPTER 1: FIRST IMPRESSIONS OF YOUR OFFICE

- You ask patients questions about their lives.
- Your patients' needs come first (blankets, water, and personalized attention).
- Everyone is honest. You trust your patients, and they trust you.
- If you don't have answers for your patients, you get them.
- Giving back to the community is a priority for your practice.
- Your office is respectful and inclusive when it comes to diversity.
- When you're running late, you apologize and never give excuses.

CHAPTER 2: WALKING INTO THE MODERN DENTAL PRACTICE

- Your office is above and beyond clean with updated (not worn) furnishings.
- The staff and doctors all pitch in for routine maintenance (light bulbs, magazines, and trash).

- You make smart investments in technology.
- Above all, you do the right thing by your patients.

CHAPTER 3: NEW PATIENT CARE

- New patients are never put on hold when they call.
- You never say no to new patients when scheduling their first appointment—even if they just get a tour and do paperwork.
- All patients are greeted by their first names right when they walk in.
- You introduce yourself by your first and last name and not as Dr. So-and-So.
- The doctor calls the new patient the night before they visit the office.
- Patients are given a Comfort Menu.
- You have a treatment coordinator—the doctor never talks money with patients.
- New patients get a tour.
- All patients are given the royal treatment.

CHAPTER 4: DENTISTS ARE AMERICA'S UNSUNG HEALTHCARE HEROES

- You believe your responsibility for patient health goes beyond the mouth and covers the whole patient.
- Your office assists in the diagnosis and prevention of many life-threatening diseases, such as hypertension, stroke, heart disease, and high blood pressure.
- You do not routinely clean teeth on a patient's very first visit.

- Patients see and hear the problem, the solution, and the consequences to not doing treatment every single time.

CHAPTER 5: BEHIND THE GREEN CURTAIN

- You never overbook appointments, except unexpected emergencies.
- You allow extra time for patients in your schedule.
- Doctors in your practice never think that the patient is on their schedule—they are on the patient's schedule.
- Patients can get guaranteed no-wait appointments.
- No more "drill, fill, and bill."
- If patients want to prepay, they get a discount.
- Offering "Groupon-level" discounts for any reason is unacceptable. You value the service you offer to patients.
- You never talk money with the patients or negotiate with them.
- You are only in competition with yourself.
- Everyone on your team pitches in—starts from the top but can be seen throughout your office.
- You have a dedicated call center or team member so patients never have to wait at your front desk to pay or make another appointment.
- Your team is always furthering their education.

CHECKLIST FOR PATIENTS: IS THIS THE RIGHT DENTIST FOR YOU?

Patients, you can use your checklist to ensure you get the best dental care available to you. Check all the boxes for which the answer is yes, yet recognize a perfect score is not realistic (not even for me).

CHAPTER 6: HOW DO YOU FEEL WHEN YOU WALK INTO YOUR DENTIST'S OFFICE?

- You trust your doctor.
- Your dentist goes above and beyond to do what's right.
- Your dentist is appreciative of referrals.
- You feel comfortable giving feedback to your dentist.
- You dentist allows you to communicate your wants, needs, and preferences.
- Your dentist takes your feedback and acts on it.
- Your dentist communicates clearly to you, and you do the same.

CHAPTER 7: GOOD, BETTER, AND GREAT EXPECTATIONS

- You can expect a high level of care from your dentist.
- You know your doctor does their best to be on time.
- The office offers guaranteed no-wait appointment times.
- Your dentist loves when you ask questions.
- Your dentist always takes the time to educate you as to the problem, the treatment, and what the consequences are if you don't do the treatment.

CHAPTER 8: HOW TO BE A GOOD PATIENT

- If you want a second opinion, your doctor helps you get the best one.
- The office has a treatment coordinator, so you never have to talk money with the dentist.
- The office is very clean, well maintained, and up to date.
- Your dentist always stresses how important your dental health is to your entire well-being.
- When you talk about new technology or methods, your dentist is very open.
- Your dentist shows you the results of your treatment.

CHAPTER 9: VETTING YOUR DENTIST

- The doctor went to a reputable dental school and/or demonstrates that continuing education is paramount to their professional growth.
- The practice gets mostly positive reviews.
- You feel encouraged to interview the entire team.
- The doctor has a wealth of experience.
- You feel like you get good value for the price of dentistry in this office.
- The dentist is not averse to referring you to a specialist or if not, explains why he or she is the best person for the procedure.
- The office culture feels positive and inclusive.
- The practice gives back to the community but isn't showy about it.
- The staff works together as a team.

Conclusion

I never thought I would write a book about dentistry, but surprisingly, this was very seamless. Now that it is done, I wonder how relevant a book on the modern dental practice will be over time because one thing is for sure, everything always changes. Just a few years ago, I

> Treat people right like a *mensch*, do the best dentistry that you can like a *maven*, and never forget to laugh (especially at yourself).

didn't even know what *millennials* were, let alone that I would have to speak an entirely different language and alter my mind-set to communicate effectively with them!

I have always wanted to use *artistic license* to excuse the fact that I often contradict myself (and announce it to the world each time!). I will now use my artistic license and contradict myself yet again. I just wrote, "Everything always changes," but I also will add, "Except the things that do not." In spite of the fact that dentistry is an ever-changing world, it is my hope that dentists' high values will never change. Treat people right like a *mensch*, do the best dentistry that you can like a *maven*, and never forget to laugh (especially at yourself). If you do those things, there is a great chance that you will have a long and rewarding career. That's what this is all about.

There's a reason I didn't include that every dentist should "do great dentistry." The fact is that you can only do the best dentistry that you can. Not every day in dentistry is going to be your greatest, and as we all know, there are many obstacles preventing a dentist from always doing "great dentistry." They say that football is a game of inches as if that's an extremely small scale of measurement. Dentists laugh at that because we deal in *fractions of millimeters* in our world. (FYI, one inch has 25.4 millimeters in it!) This is a much tighter space with a smaller margin for error, like the smallest distance you can indicate with your thumb and forefinger without them touching. And we're dealing with fractions of that millimeter every time that we place our fingers in a patient's mouth. If we are a quarter of a millimeter off, we leave a gap in between a patient's teeth. If we do a crown and it's off by a half of a millimeter, that's horrible dentistry. This is the world that we work in, and thus it is almost impossible to deliver greatness each and every time, but we can always do the best that we are capable of doing. No excuses.

The world outside the tiny one we dentists work in is so much bigger. Yet that big world is more concerned with things like cost and time, not the fractions of millimeters that we often stress over. What I've attempted to do in this book is to somehow find a place where those two worlds—our tiny one and our patient's big one—can come together.

When I first started writing this book, I asked myself, *God, am I going to be able to come up with enough material to write this book?* What I've found is that every single day I go to work, I get enough material to write another chapter! For example, I completed an Invisalign case today on Jamie, who is a professional truck driver. He told me how much his treatment has changed his life by giving him confidence. He's a single guy, and he can't believe the impact this has had on him approaching the ladies. He told me, "This has literally changed my life! Women are asking me to go out with them, and prior to you changing my smile, those same women would not even talk to me or look at me."

Right after that, I walked out of the room and almost bumped into an eighty-seven-year-old patient who has been coming to my practice for the past twenty-five years. He doesn't have a lot of money, but I "do the right thing by him." I finished his treatment that day, and I thought he had gone home. Ten minutes later he returned and asked me to come out of the treatment room, as he needed to tell me something very, very important. He took me aside and said, "Dr. Mars, I've been going to dentists for sixty or seventy years now. You're the best dentist I've ever met in my entire life. But more importantly, you're a nice person." I couldn't believe it. He was on his way home and turned around just to share this with me. This is the reason I do my job. It's people who appreciate what we're doing for them. For patients like these, those big world measurements such as cost and time don't matter very much. They get it. And it's patients like these who allow us to swallow hard and move on from those that are not so nice (a.k.a. nasty people, PIA patients, nightmare patients, etc.).

What we do in our modern practice is so much more than give people pretty smiles. We're literally changing the lives of our patients and changing the lives of our team members. It's a huge responsibility. From the eighty-seven-year-old man to the truck driver to compassionately dealing with our team members—that's how I measure professional success—not by how many dollars I collect. I have always felt that financial success will always follow and not vice versa.

The bridge between those two worlds—the big world our patients live in and the tiny one we work in—is kindness and compassion; in other words, it's relationships. In writing this book, I've attempted to bridge that gap. If I made one dentist better with this book, and if I was able to change a patient's experience for the better, then I've bridged the gap and accomplished my objective. Lastly, if I offended anyone along the way in writing this book (and I am sure I have), as you don't agree with my perspective, please accept my sincere apology and then consider how you would do it better. Then write me an email or give me a call. I would love to hear from you. By the way, in case you were wondering, names have been changed to protect the innocent and guilty and to honor my friends and relatives.

Good luck cavity fighters and patients that we serve!

.